CW01270148

Trevor Dalton
227, Burnley Rd
Colne

John Laycock

Weaver & Organbuilder

Bryan Hughes

John Laycock

WEAVER & ORGANBUILDER

Bryan Hughes

John Laycock 1808 – 1889

MUSICAL OPINION LIMITED

Published by
Musical Opinion Limited
2 Princes Road, St Leonards on Sea, East Sussex TN37 6EL

Copyright © Bryan Hughes

All rights reserved

Without limiting the rights under copyright reserved above, no part of this publication may be reproduced, stored in or introduced into a retrieval system, or transmitted in any form or by any means (electronic, mechanical, photocopied, recorded or otherwise) without prior permission of both the copyright holder and the above publisher of the book.

Printed and Bound by GH Graphics (Hastings) Ltd

ISBN: 0-9544074-0-7

Book design by Chris Monk, Yellowduck Design and Illustration
Cover photograph Bryan Hughes
John Laycock's Trade Plate, St Leonard's Church, Langho, Lancs

Contents

9   *Chapter 1*   Laicocke

13 *Chapter 2*   John Laycock 1808-1889

51 *Chapter 3*   Laycock & Bannister

94   Genealogy

To Ian Latta and Monica Price, without whose help this work would not have been possible.

ACKNOWLEDGMENTS

The authors grateful thanks are extended to the following people who so willingly gave their time and shared their memories, John Proctor; Kenneth Seward; David Smith and the late David Rhodes and William Pierce (ex-employees of Messrs. Laycock & Bannister, Crosshills, West Yorkshire). Messrs. Thompsons (Woodturners, Sutton, Crosshills. West Yorkshire.) Alan Clough; Clare Ackroyd (West Closes). Miss M Kenyon (Martin Top Chapel, Rimington, Lancashire). The staff of Barnoldswick, Colne and Skipton Libraries. W. Neville Blakey, (Photographs and Archive Material). Eileen R. Leedam; Robert Wilson Laycock; Jane Mansergh (Curator Skipton Museum). The Three Graces Masonic Lodge, Haworth, Yorks. Alan Hull (Oakworth Grammar School). W.R. Mitchell. Mr & Mrs J Ratcliffe 'Grey Court' Reedley, Burnley; David John Hawthorn; Phillip & Ann Snowdon; David M Buckroyd. MA. Oxon., (Ermysteads Grammar School, Skipton, Yorks). Eric J Mason, Organbuilder, Bolton Lancashire, Evelyn Mary Moore (Company Secretary, 1928-38 Messrs. Laycock & Bannister, Organbuilders, Crosshills). Margaret M Lyon; The clergy and custodians of the following buildings for their permission to photograph The Meeting House, Bingley, Yorks. St James'. Altham, Lancashire. Langthwaite and Gunnerside Methodist Chapels Swaledale, North Yorks. St. Nicholas' P.C. Sabden, Lancashire. Bolton Abbey, Yorks. St. Leonard's P.C. Langho, Lancashire. Scartop Sunday School, Stanbury West Yorks. St. Michael's P.C. Foulridge, Lancashire. St. John's P.C. Read, Lancashire. The Glusburn Institute, West Yorks. St. John's P.C. Nelson, Lancashire. St. Joseph's Catholic Church, Keighley, Yorks. Cedric William Laycock, Organbuilder, great grandson of John Laycock the founder.

CHAPTER ONE

Laicocke

EARLY TUDOR CRAVEN IN THE 1500S WAS WILD RUGGED YORKSHIRE MOORLAND, the forests had an abundance of Spruce and Larch and a good supply of English Oak. The plundering of English hardwood had just begun, in order to build ships for the defence of the realm. This desolate area of Yorkshire was populated by a scattering of farms, hamlets and villages; sheep and other cattle roamed at will and it was to be many years hence before the Enclosure Acts would restrict the freedom of their grazing rights. This part of West Yorkshire has retained its rugged grandeur to the present time, but in that early period of Tudor Yorkshire the ancient family of Laycock had laid down its roots.

The family of Laycock is, perhaps, one of the oldest residential families in the parish of Kildwick. The name frequently occurs as 'Laicocke' in the early registers of the parish church. In 1671, Robert Laicocke and William Laicocke were churchwardens. The townships they represented are not shown but, most probably, Glusburn, Cowling or Cononley districts would be under their jurisdiction.

The ancient title of Churchwarden carried with it a great deal of authority. They were not merely 'dog-whippers' or persons who stealthily walked the church aisles using their staffs to tap the heads of those who had fallen asleep during the hour long sermons. This practice, known as 'dobbing' caused some embarrassment to the culprit and many an argument outside the church. Nor were they elected to scour the local inns, making sure that only bonafide travellers were taking refreshment during the hours of divine service.

Throughout this period and, indeed, in some areas until well into the 18th century, parish affairs were conducted by the clergy, the four churchwardens, the parish clerk and the twenty four sidesmen. These officials were elected by the Vestry from amongst the most responsible men in the parish, whose duty it was to assist the churchwardens and to act as a sort of parish council. There were also the four overseers of the poor and the overseers of the highways. The four churchwardens were elected on Easter Tuesday of each year. They were not necessarily landowners, they could be 'Estates Men' e.g. farmers or millers. The Overseers of the Poor were also elected on Easter Tuesday and served for a term of one year, as it was not unusual for a retiring churchwarden to become an overseer; they received no payment for this duty until 1801. Overseers of the Highways, however, were renumerated and elected on St Stephen's Day, December 26th.

The Laycocks, at this time, lived off the land as farmers, yeomen or labourers. The records of the Yorkshire Archeological Society mention in the accounts of 'Early Tudor Craven' – Subsidies and Accounts of 1510-1545:

Weaver and Organ Builder 9

| 1522 | Richard Lawcoke owing to Roger Tempest | 10s (ten shillings) (50p) |
| 1522 | John Laycoke owing to Thomas Langton | 8s (eight shillings) (40p) |

In 1525, the subsidy for the Wapentake of Staincliffe, Villat (village) of Collying.[1]

1543	Miles Laycoke owing	20s-6d ($102^{1}/_{2}$p)
	Christofer Lacoke owing	40s-4d ($204^{1}/_{2}$p)
1543	Robert Lacok	40s-2d ($202^{1}/_{2}$p)

Alongside farming, handloom weaving was a cottage industry of equal importance, the income from this provided a large portion of the family's collective earnings. The early growth of this cottage industry was due to the relative freedom in Yorkshire from the Elizabethan and Stuart regulations of trade and industry which, in the incorporated towns, were imposed by the trade guilds. These rules were meant to impose restrictions of industrial development on the county districts and consisted of, for example, the Weavers. Act of 1558 and The Statute of Apprenticeship of 1563. These statutes laid down limits as to the number of looms a county weaver was allowed to own and the number of years he must serve as an apprentice and at the end of this period to be awarded with a recognised status of having served a period of training.[2]

In Lancashire and the West Riding of Yorkshire, these acts did not apply: free from regulations, handloom weavers flourished alongside farming and other trades. Almost every household had its loom. Many farmers owned two or three looms, depending upon the number of persons in the household who were capable of carrying out this type of work. Generally, the husband and male members of the family farmed the land. The churning, cheese making and other household duties were the responsibility of wives, daughters and female servants; they also carried out the necessary preparations prior to weaving the finished product. If the farmer owned the freehold of his land and was rich enough to own several sheep to supply his needs, carry out his own shearing and to employ a number of weavers, then all the processing of the raw material would be carried out at the 'home farm'. This process included slubbing and spinning the wool and afterwards forming it into warps for the loom. However, this sort of establishment was not often found in this area of West Yorkshire.

In 17th century Yorkshire, a farmer would pay the rent for his 'holding' from one or other branch of trade such as spinning and weaving. Other households, too, made a livelihood from the handloom; this they would reluctantly leave for a few weeks only to help with the harvest. A cottage rent in the 1780s was £1-10s-0d per annum (150p), which included a room or outbuilding for weaving and a small plot of land for the provision of vegetables. A weaver could earn from eight shillings (40p) to ten shillings (50p) per week. Should he have a son or an assistant to share the work he would be paid around six shillings per week (30p). With such low earnings the cottage weavers could not afford to lay out money for their raw material (yarn). This was provided by a supplier known as a 'putter out', who would organise the spinning of the yarn and in some cases the dyeing, the weaver being required to produce the patterns. The coloured material was known as 'grey' (Greige) or 'ecru'. Other workers were known as 'dressers', their task being to split off the lengths of the soft coil warp yarn depending on the amount of colour required. The woven cloth pieces were then returned to the 'putter out' who paid the weavers for their work and arranged for the pieces to be finished. This finishing process was known as 'lanting', one such method being to dip the pieces of woven cloth in urine, after which it was trampled upon in order to increase its density. This was then followed by another process of washing and cleansing.[3]

The weavers stiffened and dressed their own warps whilst it was fixed in the loom frame. This was done by applying a 'size' with a flat brush to the stretched material. The 'size' paste was a mixture of flour and water boiled in a pan over the open kitchen fire. The paste was then stored for future use in a stone trough known as a 'sow-box.' A length of cloth approximately six feet long would be treated at one time, hot irons, possibly 'flat' irons used for laundering would then be applied to dry out the warp. A stiff paper was held over the damp warp to prevent an over heated iron from damaging the material.[4]

In 1722, a weaver would receive £1-2s-0d (110p) for forty yards of cloth woven on a handloom.[5] At the end of the next two decades there was a period of 'Distress'; this affected the weavers in both Yorkshire and Lancashire. In the village of Higham, near Padiham, Lancashire, the records show there were one hundred and three handloom weavers earning a weekly wage of two shillings (10p). The staple diet of these artisans was oatmeal and with the cost of a 4lb loaf at one shilling two and a half pence, they were almost at starvation level.[6]

Between this period and the development of the 'factory system' John Laycock was born in 1808. By now the wages of handloom weavers had been considerably reduced and the cottage weaving industry gradually declined over the following fifty years. One by one the cottage looms ceased working, the weavers moving into towns or cities to work in the mills.

In villages such as Kildwick, Crosshills and Haworth the end of the handloom weaving era was much slower than in other areas.

Fig.1. John Laycock 1808 – 1899

John Laycock, in his early youth, was to experience life at the closing stages of the cottage weaving industry, to which he became apprenticed. Later, he, too, was to leave the trade in order to develop his talents in a completely different craft.

Chapter 1 Laicocke
References
1. Yorkshire Archeological Society Records
2. A History of the Lancashire Cotton Industry. Edwin Hopwood
3. Ibid
4. Ibid
5. Ibid
6. Ibid

CHAPTER TWO
John Laycock 1808-1889

In 1803, William Laycock (1780-1865) brought Ann Wilson as his wife to Cook house, West Closes, Near Crosshills, West Yorkshire. Here he farmed the land, keeping a few cattle and supplementing his weekly income by handloom weaving. His pieces of cloth would be sold in Crosshills or carried by pack horse to the Cloth Halls in Colne or Heptonstall.

Today, Cook House remains in its isolation, a single terraced cottage, built of stone with outbuildings and boundary walling from the same local material. The dwelling is cut off from the main roadway and access is by way of an old cart track and thence by an uphill walk across rough pastureland and over a rebuilt stile.

This area, known as West Closes, Glusburn, near Crosshills, West Yorkshire, retains much of its rugged character, its sense of timelessness, its natural grandeur. In the lower levels, the forest, now not so dense as in earlier times, is still much in evidence with the beck still making its way through this wooded stretch from the higher villages of Lothersdale, Ickornshaw and Glusburn. In the bottom of the valley the township of Crosshills appears just to have happened over the years, as each building was added alongside its neighbour. The winding lanes from the town leading to West Closes follow the old cart tracks edged with rough cut dry stone walling, the line of drip-stones testifying to the skill of the old 'wallers'. This is an area of scattered farms having been worked by generations of farming families and inherited from grandfathers through to grandsons.

On November 24th, 1808, the first and only child was born to William and Ann Laycock at Cook House, West Closes, Glusburn, West Yorkshire, a son, John, baptised in Kildwick Parish Church; John – Born 1808. Died September 13th, 1889.[1]

During John's brief years at school he managed to learn the rudiments of the 'three Rs' under the tuition of Mr Wilcock of Crosshills. In these early years John was kept busy helping his father with various tasks around the smallholding, rounding up the cattle, cleaning the byre and, during the haymaking season would no doubt miss his school lessons, as every hand, however small, was of use at this time. Young John was also a contemporary of the Brontes, who lived over the intervening moors in Haworth and, also, of Timmy Feather, the famous handloom weaver of neighbouring Stanbury.

The ancient craft of handloom weaving was by this time in a state of decline. Those who owned small workplaces with only a few employees soon discovered that handlooms were no match against the performances of the power looms operated by steam in the factory system. As a consequence of this, the earnings of those remaining in the 'old craft' were drastically reduced.

Weaver and Organ Builder 13

The Kildwick Parish registers record, however, that for the next twenty years there were fourteen small manufacturers working in the 'old way,' three of these producing worsted material.

Handloom weaving was an occupation of the Laycock family, as important as farming and a means of supplementing a weekly income. At an early age John Laycock was apprenticed as a handloom weaver, as the industry was still prominent in the Lower Airedale. Whether young John was apprenticed to a cottage weaver or to a small workshop employer is not known. If he ever attained any excellence in this work has never been revealed and seems doubtful, his mind being occupied with other things such as mechanics, physics and music. No doubt he was encouraged in this respect, either by his parents or with some help from the local blacksmith. Certainly, some music lessons had been arranged for him or he may have been taught by a member of the family because, later, he played the flute in a small band which provided music to accompany the services at Kildwick Parish Church.

This fine building of late 15th and early 16th century architecture is some 160 feet from east to west (49 metres) and is known as 'Lang Kirk O'Craven', but it was many years before John Laycock was to make music his full time career. Meanwhile, he became more and more absorbed in things mechanical. He still made his livelihood at the loom but seemed to have little heart for the work. His insatiable urge to create things would, on occasion, cause the 'clash' of his shuttle to cease whilst he added another part to the waterwheel or some other mechanical gadget.[2]

Later, he became apprenticed to his uncle George, who worked as a Cartwright. Now he was able to gain more experience in fashioning things made from wood and metal.[3] He was taught how to obtain the correct curve for the 'follys' when making the wheels for farm carts, the making of spokes and obtaining the correct 'dish' and how to turn the centre hub of a wheel. This latter may have been turned on a 'pole lathe' or the machine could have been powered by a foot treadle. Alternatively, the headstock could have been rotated by a larger wheel attached to a smaller pulley of the headstock; the larger wheel was then rotated by hand power. There would also be innumerable jobs to be carried out around the farm buildings in the area. Gates and doors would need constant repair, together with mechanical parts of farming machinery. His hours of recreation were spent making models and in his love of music.

In 1837, John Laycock married his first wife, Ann Proctor. Between this date and 1841, John, with his wife and young family moved from Cook House to West Closes, only a short distance away, taking with them his parents, his uncle George and two servants. Some of the immediate family were left behind. The Glusburn Census for 1841 (Leeds Central Reference Library) provides the names of inhabitants living at Cook House.[4]

William Laycock	*Aged 60*	Farmer
Ann Laycock	*Aged 60*	Wife
George Laycock (uncle)	*Aged 70*	Wheelwright
Robert Laycock	*Aged 65*	Labourer
Jane	*Aged 8*	

John Laycock	*Aged 30*	Wheelwright
Ann Laycock (nee Proctor)	*Aged 35*	Wife
George Laycock	*Aged 25*	Weaver
Martha Laycock	*Aged 20*	
Mary Laycock	*Aged 30.*	

John Laycock's move from Cook House to West Closes appears to have been brought about by a common problem in the 1800s, one of overcrowding. Apart from this problem he undoubtedly had other plans.

West Closes is situated only a short distance from Cook house and is separated only by stone boundary walls. The house itself is built of local stone, as are the few out buildings. There is also a large well built stone barn, its roof supported by an oak Queen Post truss. From this building John Laycock was to launch out upon his new career.

The Census for 1841 confirms that John Laycock was still making his living as a wheelwright and that he had taken some members of the Laycock family with him to West Closes; included among them was his uncle George, now aged seventy.

Fig. 2. Cook House, Glusburn, West Yorkshire. Birthplace of John Laycock.

Fig. 3. West Closes, Glusburn, Crosshills. Yorks. John Laycock moved here with his family to begin life as an organbuilder, the 'organ gallery' workshop is close by.

The 1841 Census, West Closes, Glusburn, West Yorkshire (Leeds Central Reference Library) reads;[5]

John Laycock	*Aged 30*	Wheelwright
Ann Laycock	*Aged 35*	Wife
Elizabeth	*Aged 5*	
George	*Aged 2*	
Robert	*Aged 3 months*	
George Laycock (uncle to John)		
	Aged 70	Wheelright.

    1839 was the turning point in John's career. A situation arose which, in future years, would make the name of Laycock well known and highly respected in the county of Yorkshire. It was in this year that the trustees of Ickornshaw Wesleyan Chapel, Cowling, West Yorkshire, removed the organ from their chapel in order to install a new one. The old instrument became the property of John Laycock for the sum of £5.00 Fascinated with its construction and mechanism he attempted to produce a similar instrument; this he sold privately. Finally, in 1840 he gave up his adopted trade as a wheelwright and established himself as an organbuilder.

    At West Closes, the spacious barn now provided a useful and lofty workshop, the tie-beams of the roof trusses were ideal for the storage of timber and there was adequate natural light. John Laycock was industrious, ingenious and conscientious. He was now establishing himself in a new business and alongside his new found craft he was obliged to use his skills in all kinds of work in order to provide a living. He was skilled with his hands and subsidised his income by making picture frames, barometers and clocks. In his workshop at West Closes was a clock which had kept perfect time for thirty-five years. Its mechanism consisted of only three wheels, two having the power of motion, the third being a balance wheel. Another example was made entirely from wood and indicated not just the hours but also the days of the month. He repaired pianos, supplied parts to looms and carried out the duties of a local undertaker. Yet in the commissions he received from various churches and chapels he was able to compete successfully with organ builders in Yorkshire and Lancashire.

JOHN LAYCOCK 1808-1889

Fig. 4. The barn known as the 'Organ Gallery" West Closes. West Yorkshire

The first instrument he built was for the Wesleyan Chapel, Crosshills, West Yorkshire. The instrument gave service for fifty-eight years when later it was rebuilt and installed in the Meeting House Chapel. Bingley, Yorks, in 1930. (Now Bingley Independent Methodist Church.)[6]

Fig. 5. The Meeting House Chapel, Bingley, Yorkshire; Now Bingley Independent Methodist Church.[6]

Fig. 6. The Meeting House Chapel, Bingley, Yorkshire, Organ was built by John Laycock originally in the Wesleyan Chapel, Crosshills. The tombstone of John Laycock's grave in Kildwick Church yard is a replica of this casework.

The first fifteen years of Laycock's organ building activities were slow to develop and, alongside organ building, he took upon himself other forms of work which came his way. He now had a family to support and a few relatives who resided with him; these were lean times in the 1850s in a rural district. John was a practical man and could turn his hands to a number of skills in order to make a living. The early shop and farming books, still extant and dating from 1833 clearly show that work on the repair of organs and pianos was carried out alongside his occupation as a wheelwright together with farming activities. The entries in the shop books are limited and instruments are simply recorded as 'organ of one or two manuals'; rarely is there a complete specification, scaling of pipe work, wind pressures or construction details recorded. In between these 'organ entries' other entries intrude of farming business and household accounts. John Laycock's Books circa.1833.[7]

1833.   Pedal Bourdon. Cut-up six cuts on lip. six inch mouth width between lips (152mm)
1833.   Pneumatic soundboard: Pedal. Valve Hole Valve Buffer Diaphragm
           CCC-FFF   2"(50mm). $2^{3/4}$"(70mm). $2^{1/2}$"(63mm). $3^{1/4}$"(82mm).
           CC-AA $1^{1/4}$"(31mm). $1^{1/2}$"(38mm). $1^{3/4}$"(44mm). $2^{1/4}$"(57mm).

1833   Nancy Scotson.   7 bushels of oats
           Widow Brown   1 stone lump flour
           John Feather Borrowed   54 lbs (pounds) of meal.

John Laycock's early years were spent at the loom, where he took an interest in the mechanism and was able to supply new parts to many weavers' looms in the local villages.

1856   John Laycock's Shop Book entry;[8]
           Repairs to weaving looms
           One new drum – two shillings 2/– (10p)
           8 thick jacks – two shillings and sixpence 2/6d ($12^{1/2}$p)
           Two treadles and brackets-one shilling 1/– (5p)
           James Laycock $^{3/4}$ of a peck of bran
           James Laycock 92 lbs (pounds) of oats.

The earliest unaltered instrument still extant of Laycock's work is to be found in the Baptist Chapel at Cowling Hill near Crosshills, Yorkshire. The chapel is built in the centre of what was once a farm yard and dates from 1742. The organ arrived at Cowling Hill, West Yorkshire in 1869. It is built in the style of an upright grand piano, an instrument that John Laycock would have seen in the large houses of some mill-owners where he had tuned the instrument or supplied various parts for their looms. The pinewood casework is in the classical design with turned and carved columns, divided 'flats' to the non-speaking façade pipes and bold crown mouldings compliment the decorated pipes. The keyboard is supported by heavy turned wooden legs, piano style: the positioning of these has, however, caused the eighteen note pedal board to be positioned out of alignment with the manual keys. The tone is pleasant but restrained and the pipe work is positioned on a common soundboard. The wind is still supplied by a hand blowing mechanism. This is a rare and early example of a chamber organ from the workshop of West Closes and still in use.

The Baptist Chapel, Cowling Hill, Cowling, Yorkshire
Chamber organ by John Laycock. 1851

Specification
Manual GG-g in alt.
Pedal coupled to Manual

Left hand stop jamb	Right hand stop jamb	
Open Diapason (Tenor f to top)	Dulciana	(tenor f to top)
Stopped Diapason	Principal	(full compass)
Stopped Diapason Bass	Fifteenth	(full compass)

Fig. 7. Cowling Hill Baptist Chapel. Cowling, Yorks. 1851 chamber organ built by John Laycock.

In any rural community there was mortality and there was always a need for someone to take care of these events. John Laycock, in his capacity as an organ repairer would have a supply of timber i.e. boarding. This he could turn to good use when the occasion arose and we find frequent references in the 'shop books' to John's undertaking activities. This was the mid nineteenth century; there was no cold storage in those days or adequate mortuary facilities. The corpse was usually laid out in the best front room of the home, or if in poor circumstances in an outbuilding at the local inn or, if need be, in a barn or stable. John was a man of his time, imbued with a rough sympathetic nature and equipped with a strong constitution. He would, no doubt, be equal to the task.

Fig. 8. Cowling Hill Baptist Chapel. Cowling, Yorks. Console of 1851 chamber Organ by John Laycock. Built in the style of an upright grand.

Account Books. Laycock 1857; [9]

    Mrs Watson – Cowling village.
    To pitch pine coffin covered with cloth and lined with flannel
    With engraved metal plate and eight handles   £4-5s-0d (£4.25p)
    To flannel shroud. Thirteen shillings   13/–   (65p)

    WB Mannion Carhead village
    Repairs to piano. Two shillings   2/–   (10p)

    Hall Green chapel, Haworth
    Organ tuning & repairs. Two shillings and sixpence   2/6d ($12^{1}/_{2}$p).

The accounts records provide an insight into the working life of a rural craftsman, how circumstances directed the necessity to diversify his skills in order to make a living. Nevertheless, farming activities still took up a large part of John Laycock's life; there are numerous entries to whom he sold bran, oats, flour, meal etc, and special notes made of those who had borrowed provisions and materials.

Gradually, the quality of his organ building became known outside his local village and with an increase in trade and other miscellaneous work, it became necessary to consider some form of mechanisation. John had built a number of waterwheels in the area; unfortunately, the water supply was too far away from the house and workshop at West Closes. The beck in the lower valley ran through the village of Ickornshaw. West Closes, situated at a much higher level, had the benefit of strong wind currents. Here he built a windmill, the sails of which had adjustable shutters and which, by a single movement of a lever caused them to open or close, thus varying the speed of the sails.[10] (This movement had a similar action to that which was required in an organ swell box and which caused the sound to either increase or diminish). To the shaft of this mill, pulleys and belts were fitted and used to power the circular saw used in the 'organ gallery.' John Laycock now had to keep an eye on the weather and to use the periods when strong winds blew to cut his timber sections and to make sure there was always enough in stock.

More work was continuing to arrive at a steady pace between 1857-60 as a sample of the shop books record: [11]

	To James Edwardson of Cowling - One weatherglass	17s-6d	(87½p)
	Picture frames	£1-15s-6d	(£1.77½p)
1858	Skipton Parish Church – Tuning organ	£2-15s-0d	(2.75p)
1859	St George's PC, Barnsley, Yorks		
	New swell Gamba G-F		
	New bellows and pedal organ	£113-10s-0d	
	Allowance for old swell organ	£12-0d-0d	

In 1860 a new organ was built for the Revd. T Hayes of Bracewell. Several instruments have occupied Bracewell Parish Church, Lancashire throughout its long history. Whether this instrument was intended for erection within the church or a private commission for this reverend gentleman's vicarage is not clear. From the existing specification it was obviously a small chamber organ having a single keyboard or manual and eight stops. Here is shown Laycock's attempt to expand his knowledge in chorus building by the inclusion of a manual 'double' and a mixture stop of three ranks of pipes.

Organ for the Revd T Hayes of Bracewell; Cost £88-0-0d.[12]	
Bourdon to middle B	
Double Open Diapason	CC-G full compass
Viole d'Gamba	Tenor C
Stopped Diapason	Bass
Principal	Full Compass
Fifteenth	Full Compass
Sesquialtera	3 ranks

This commission was followed by another for the Revd N Fawcett of Morten, West Yorks who ordered a new Dulciana stop for his church organ and gave him the care and maintenance of the instrument. A mixture of work was to follow which is included in the records:[13]

1861	William Shuttleworth of Cowling; Work on bobbin engine	1s-3d	(6½p)
1861	Whittaker. Lumb Mill, Rossendale		
	5 setts of heads and shaft 40 feet	5s-0d	(25p)
1861	Eccleshall Parish Church. Yorks. Enlarging organ	£39-0s-0d	

In some rural establishments servants were provided with items of clothing. This may have been part of an agreement of employment or costs repaid by small deductions from wages. Account Book.1861 July – To Sarah Bugget[14]

Three pairs of felt shoes	7s-6d	(37½p)
Two pairs of stockings	3s-6d	(17½p)
Black silk mantle	£1-5s-0d	(£1.25p)
One pair of stays	4s-6d	(22½p)

The above items would be expected to last for a year. The black mantle, undoubtedly for best wear-attendance at church or it might be that the servant, Sarah Bugget, was the one who visited the homes of the bereaved and laid out the corpse; therefore, a good black mantle would be something of a status symbol.

Account Book. 1861. November;[15]
Peter Barrett of Eastburn
   Coffin, pitch pine covered with cloth and lined   £4-12s-0d   (£4.60p)
David Fernharts of Weaver Green
   Coffin of pitch pine with best black plate   £4-5s-1d   (£4.25p)
   Shroud   4s-6d   (22½p)
David Wormall –
   Oak coffin, lined, black plate and eight handles   £4-5s-6d (£4.27½p)
   Shroud   4s-6d   (22½p)

After some years in the workshop at West Closes, John Laycock suffered a severe accident, when he lost the fingers of his left hand, whilst using the circular saw. His foreman, Charles Bannister, rushed to the house for bandages and succeeded in binding back the finger stumps. The bandages were then coated with glue to make a seal and remained so for almost a year. During this time John never missed a day's work. When the bandages were finally removed it was discovered that the 'stumps' had grafted themselves on to the fingers and remained so until the end of Laycock's life. He used his left hand as support when using the tools of his craft. [16]

At West Closes John Laycock formed a small debating society and technical school (it would be known in those days as an 'evening class'.) They were held in the 'organ gallery' barn or, alternatively, at one of the farm houses. These evening meetings encouraged the youth of the area to join in with discussions on various topics and to acquire some basic knowledge of geometry, physics and mathematics.[17]

Johns love of music led him to make frequent visits to the nearest city, Leeds, where he could hear professional performers. Here, in 1842, the new parish church of St. Peter had been built to a design in the Gothic style by the architect Dennis Chantrel. Dr. Theodore Farquhar Hook had become Vicar of Leeds, where he instituted and encouraged a fully choral service and was insistent upon a high standard of musicianship, a tradition which has prevailed to the present time. Dr Hook had engaged as his organist Dr. Samuel Sebastian Wesley, who had held organists posts at Hereford, Exeter and Winchester Cathedrals. He was a member of that renowned family who included in their number Charles Wesley, the hymn writer and the famous John Wesley of the Methodist Church.[18]

At Leeds Parish Church, Samuel Sebastian Wesley played to packed congregations who came to hear his out-going voluntaries and his recitals. John Laycock was among those who attended these occasions and, before the coming of the railways, he would rise early on Sunday mornings in order to walk the twenty five miles to Leeds Parish Church, where he could immerse himself in Wesley's organ playing and the beauty of the choral singing.

St. Bartholomew's Parish Church
Colne, Lancashire

On a map of 1610 Colne appears as one of the fifteen largest towns in the County of Lancaster. Ecclesiastically it was one of seven original chapelries of the ancient Parish of Whalley. The Colne parish registers date back to 1599, but the early history of the church of St Bartholomew's may be traced back to 1515. The church has undergone several restorations throughout its long history and a major restoration took place in 1857. At this time the organ and choir gallery (erected in 1833) which blocked the tower arch was removed and a new North aisle and organ chamber were provided. In 1889, a further restoration was carried out to the designs of the Architects Austin & Paley of Lancaster. They removed the north aisle, replacing it with a double north aisle in keeping with the rest of the building and also placed an organ chamber at its east end. At this period, also, the ancient chancel screen was removed and re-positioned and the present screen erected.

Until the end of the 19th century various benches in the church dating back to 1703, were occupied regularly by farmers from all parts of the chapelry. A common sight was to see a farmer taking a bundle of straw into the church, where it was spread under his seat to keep his feet warm on the following Sunday.[19]

The bells of Colne Church are mentioned from an early date and the present ring of eight are the descendants of a long succession of bells. Six of the present ring were cast by Mears of Whitechapel, London in 1814 and came out of their moulds as a 'Maiden Peal' i.e in perfect tune. Transportation was by sea from London to Hull, then via the Leeds & Liverpool canal to Foulridge, where the remainder of the journey was by horse drawn conveyance.

Early music in Colne parish Church was provided by a bassoon and a clarinet. In 1778 the chuchwardens paid one shilling (5p) for a pitch pipe from London. By 1815, an organ had been acquired and erected in the west gallery; of this instrument there is no further information except that it was removed in 1856/7. [20]

John Laycock was now commissioned to provide an instrument for this historical church, which was erected in the western gallery: when this was later removed the instrument was transferred to an organ chamber on the north east side of the building.

Built by John Laycock of West Closes, Glusburn, West Yorks. 1856-7:

Great. CC-F 54 notes		**Swell. CC-F 54 notes**	
Double Open Diapason	16' metal	Double Open Diapason	16' wood
Double Open Diapason	16' metal	Open Diapason	8' metal
		Diapason	8' wood
Dulciana	8' metal	Principal	4' metal
Claribel Flute Treble	8' wood	Fifteenth	2' metal
Stopped Diapason Bass	8' wood	Mixture	III rks metal
Viol di Gamba	8' metal	Cornopean	8' metal
Claribel Flute	4' wood	Hautboy	8' metal
Principal	4' metal	Clarion	4' metal
Twelfth	2 2/3 metal		
Fifteenth	2' metal	**Couplers**	
Sesquialtera	III ranks metal		
Trumpet	8' metal	Swell to Great	
Trumpet Bass	8' metal	Great to Pedal	
Clarion	4' metal	Keys to change Pedal Pipes	
Cremona	8' metal	5 combination pedals	
Pedal. CCC-E		Hand blowing mechanism	
Grand Open Diapason	16' wood		

From the recorded specification it appears to have been a very ambitious instrument from the workshops of a rural craftsman. On the Great or main keyboard there is a Diapason Chorus from 16ft to Sesquialtera mixture; this would give a singing quality to the tonal structure; a flute chorus at 8ft and 4ft pitches, a string gamba and reeds again at 8ft and 4ft pitch with one 8ft reed divided for use as both a chorus and solo voice. On the swell organ (second keyboard) is a secondary diapason or main chorus and also a chorus of reedwork at 8ft-8ft-4ft pitches. The drawstop labelled 'Keys to Change Pedals' is thought to have been a mechanism to bring the Grand pedal Diapason onto the Great keyboard to be played by the fingers, This instrument underwent some modification between 1889-91 by Laycock and Bannister of Crosshills, Yorks. At this time the pedal section was enlarged but the instrument remained basically in its original state and enclosed in its casework of panelled oak. The excellence of this instrument probably led to the commission John Laycock received in 1880 to build an organ for Bolton Abbey.

The Laycock instrument at Colne lasted until 1909 when it was replaced by a more 'modern one' equipped with some of the latest mechanical aids and action. This was built by Messrs. Brindley and Foster of Sheffield, who installed it in John Laycock's casework.

The Church at the Ford

The foundation of the ancient church at Altham, Lancashire, dates back to the reign of Stephen (1135-1154). Hugh the Saxon built a 'church at the ford', which might have been a simple hermitage. There were continuing squabbles for the rights to appoint the clergy to Altham. Finally, in 1249 AD St James' was judged to be an independent chapelry to the Rector of Whalley.

During the 14th century the small Norman church was reconstructed in the Gothic style and the elaborate tracery of the eastern window in the north aisle is from this period.[21]

The present church, in the perpendicular style was built in the early part of the 15th century. The 12th century Norman font is incorporated into the corner of the western porch; part of it has been chiselled away to form a seat and is reputed to be the oldest example of its kind in the north west of England: in this font the early Lords of Altham were baptised.

The stained glass is of interest, a painted window to the memory of John Hackory, inventor of the Carding Engine, a process which aligned the fibres of new wool or cotton. The east window is the work of Whitefriars Glass of London and bears their logo, a small white friar.[22]

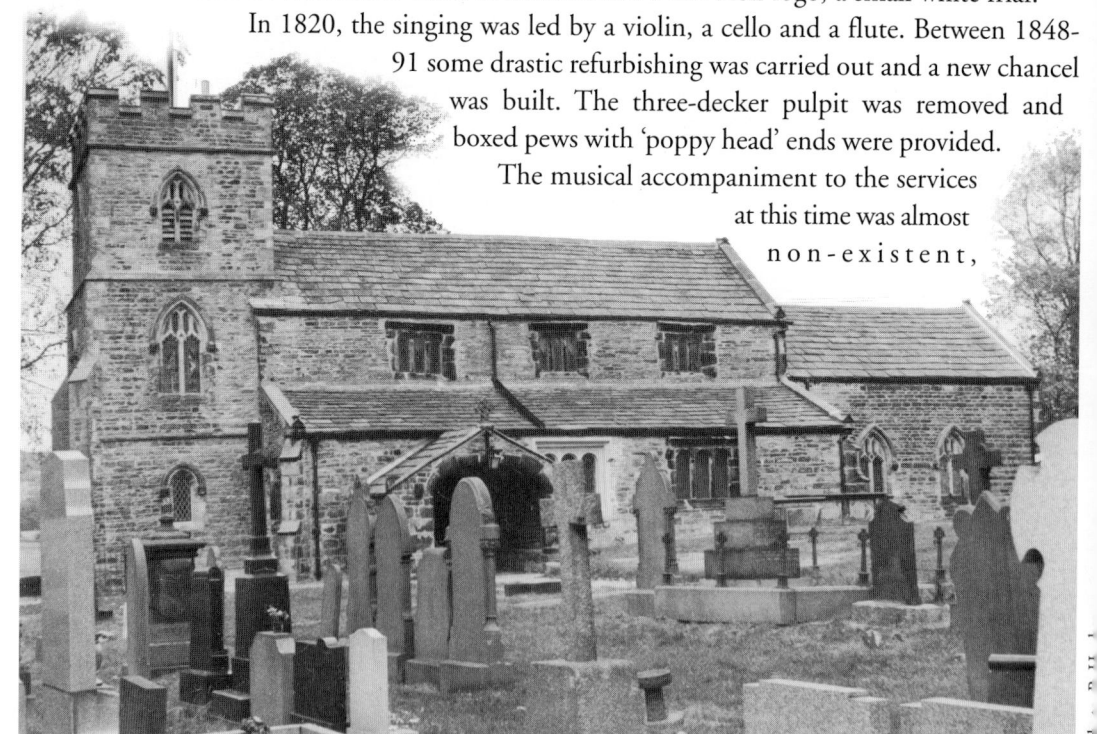

In 1820, the singing was led by a violin, a cello and a flute. Between 1848-91 some drastic refurbishing was carried out and a new chancel was built. The three-decker pulpit was removed and boxed pews with 'poppy head' ends were provided. The musical accompaniment to the services at this time was almost non-existent,

Fig.9. The Parish Church of St. James', Altham. Lancashire.

having been reduced to a single bass fiddle. This was replaced temporarily by what is described as 'a small organ' positioned behind the pulpit; this appears to indicate either a chamber organ or harmonium. When the belfry was replaced at the west end of the church by the rebuilding of the tower, space was provided for a west end organ gallery.

The commission to build an organ for St. James', Altham, was awarded to John Laycock and was completed in 1862. It is an example of how a rural craftsman can overcome the difficulties of limited space in a western gallery and is an early example of Laycock's larger church organ. The voicing of the pipe work has the 'singing' quality one associates with the early English organ. The pedal section is unusual with the inclusion of a fifth which draws with the Pedal Bourdon 16ft slide. Here Laycock is including a harmonic which he has discovered will provide a clearer musical line in the bass; something he may have grasped from his days in the church orchestra. Another unusual form of construction is in the pipe ranks where, on the Great or main organ several ranks are not of full compass (known as Tenor C. stops) i.e the bass octaves having the

Fig. 10. St. James' Parish Church, Altham, Lancashire. 1862 instrument built by John Laycock in the west gallery.

Fig. 11. St. James' Parish Church, Altham, Lancashire. Console of organ. In the west gallery built by John Laycock 1862.

longest pipes omitted and a single bass rank has been provided for all of them. This was done to overcome the restricted height in the west gallery. Nevertheless, tonally the instrument fits the building and has some very fine chorus work; both church and organ are worthy of a visit.

Fig. 12. St. James' Parish Church, Altham Lancashire. Organ built 1862. Stop jambs. Note the highlight marking to the drawstop faces. Frequently used by John Laycock.

St. James' Parish Church, Altham Lancashire

Organ built by John Laycock at West Closes 'organ gallery.' 1862. Specification.

Manuals CC-G: Pedals CCC-E

Great **Pedal**
Open Diapason (Tenor. C.) Open Diapason 16ft
Viola di Gamba (Tenor. C.) Pedal Fifth
Stopped. Diapason (Bass to tenor C. stops) Pedal Octave
Clarabella (Tenor. C.)
Principal
Harmonic Flute (Tenor. C.) **Couplers**
Fifteenth Swell to Great
Cremona (Tenor. C.) Great to Pedal
Cornopean Bass

Swell
Double Diapason
Open Diapason
Voix Celeste
Keraulophon
Stopped Diapason
Principal (Tenor. C. Bass from Stopped Diapason)
Piccolo (Tenor. C. Bass from Stopped Diapason)
Cornopean (Tenor. C. Bass from Stopped Diapason)
Hautboy (Tenor. C. Bass from Stopped Diapason)

3 Combination pedals to Great
2 Combination pedals to Swell
Flat pedal board with slight radiation

After completing the work at Altham, there followed an order for a small organ of one keyboard and a handful of stops for the Wesleyan Sunday School, Keighley, costing £45. Tuning and maintenance at Cowling Primitive Chapel and the overhauling and cleaning of the organ at Trinity Church, Ripon, all took place in 1863. This work would not, however, provide enough income to support the family. It clearly explains the diversity of entries in the account books for, in the same year, we find:

John Laycock. Account Book.[23]

To the Churchwardens, Kildwick. Repairing clock	2s-6d (12½p)
Picture Frames	£1-0s-0d (100p)
Repairing pianoforte	2s 0d (10p)

Mr John Wilson. Lothersdale & Crosshills Shop (Loom repairs)
48 Jacks

36 Pulleys	2s-0d	(10p)
1 New Drum	2s-6d	(12½p)
8 Thick Jacks		
New stoppers and springing staves	8d	(4p)
2 treadles and brackets	8s-0d	(40p)

Before the railway had been brought to Crosshills, John Laycock transported the organs he built by horse-drawn conveyance. The finished instrument would be erected in the 'organ gallery' at West Closes. After being checked that all was in working order it was dismantled and the sections loaded on to a farmer's flat cart, covered with sheets and securely roped into place. We might imagine the scene in the cobbled area around the barn or 'organ gallery' at West Closes. The shire horses brushed, harnesses and brasses polished, John would wish to create a good impression both on the road and during the unloading at the church. It was a form of advertisement. The eventual progression of the railways did not preclude the use of horse transport. One instrument, bound for the village chapel of Langthwaite in Arkengarthdale in the Yorkshire Dales was sent by rail from Crosshills to Richmond. There it was met by several large harvest carts, all double harnessed with shire horses. After the various sections and crates had been transferred from railway platform to farm carts the 'grand procession' moved off from Richmond Station to cover the 15-20 miles to their destination. As darkness approached, oil lamps were lit and attached to the sides of the carts. The sight of this cavalcade in the evening light bringing in the chapel organ and the villagers lining the main street awaiting its arrival, became a talking point for many months and an occasion which has, fortunately, been recorded for posterity.

Fig. 13. Langthwaite Methodist Chapel, North Yorkshire. Two manuals and pedals with twelve stops.

Photo. B. Hughes

Langthwaite Methodist Church, Arkengarthdale

Organ built by John Laycock
Manuals. CC-G: Pedals CCC-F

Great		**Swell**		**Pedal**	
Open Diapason	8'	Violin Diapason	8'	Bourdon	16'
Dulciana	8'	Salicional	8'	Bass Flute	8'
Hohl Flute	8'	Lieblich Gedackt	8'		
Principal	4'	Oboe	8'		
		Tremulant			

Couplers
Swell to Great
Swell to Pedal
Great to Pedal

2 combination pedals to Great & Pedal
2 combination pedals to Swell
Mechanical action
Pitch pine casework

A similar instrument was built for the Methodist Chapel in the village of Gunnerside, Swaledale. This rather large village is situated on a broad hillside formed by Gunnerside Gill which sweeps down from Rogans' Seat (2,204 ft). The bottom of the dale has irregular ancient enclosures. Many of the village dwellings are the homes of families who worked the Old Gang mines – these were lead mines, the lead was carried by pack horse down the dale where it was taken southwards and sold overseas.

Gunnerside Chapel was built in 1866, a solid square single cell structure, galleried on three sides. Here, as at Langthwaite, Laycock is providing an instrument for the accompaniment of hymn tunes, there is an abundance of unison pitch giving foundational tone and in this larger chapel he provides an extra Flute 4ft stop on the Great and a sharp toned string named Gamba on the second keyboard. The casework is a simple polished framework with the stencilled facade pipework alleviating a plain frontal.

Gunnerside Methodist Chapel, Swaledale

Organ built by John Laycock
13 stops. Manuals CC-A: Pedal CCC-F

Great		**Swell**		**Pedal**	
Open Diapason	8'	Violin Diapason	8'	Bourdon	16'
Dulciana	8'	Gedact	8'	Bass Flute	8'
Clarabella	8'	Gamba	8'		
Principal	4'	Voix Celeste	8'		
Flute	4'	Oboe	8'		
		Tremulant			

Couplers 2 combination pedals to Great
Swell to Great Mechanical action
Great to Pedal
Swell to Pedal

Fig. 14. Gunnerside Chapel, Swaledale, Yorks. Built 1866.

John Laycock became competent as a woodturner, he had provided his lathe with an eccentric chuck, entirely his own design. With this modification he could produce geometrical carvings and patterns of delicate workmanship. Specimens of his turned work in the form of snuff boxes and tobacco boxes; egg cups and wooden bowls were frequent gifts to friends and contributions to bazaars held for charitable organisations. He never cared to make a monetary profit from the objects he produced on his lathe, he seemed simply to be happy with the pleasure he gave to others through his skill. He had a remarkable artistic sensitivity, and the results of this are several landscape paintings.

In 1867 two new organs were produced. The first was built for Sion Chapel, Burnley and cost £315-0-0d; the old instrument was removed to the Wesleyan Sunday School, Oswaldtwistle. It is the second of these two instruments, built for Martin Top Salem Congregational Chapel, Rimington, Lancashire which provides an interesting story of the events surrounding this chapel, its location and some of the village people who helped it to thrive.

During the reign of George III in 1816 the friends connected with the 'meeting house' at Martin Top, Rimington, Lancashire were anxious to begin to build their chapel. An area of land had been acquired but before building could begin £500 was required to complete the total cost

Fig. 15. Gunnerside Chapel, Swaledale. Yorks. Organ built by John Laycock.

Fig. 16. Turned ebony snuff box with engraved lid. The work of John Laycock.

of the chapel. The chapel was opened in 1817. The congregation flourished and by 1836 cottages had been erected on the eastern side. In order to pay the builders a local handloom weaver had suggested that if twenty trustees were to loan £25 each, free of interest, for a period of three years the problem would be solved. Another member, Francis Holgate, borrowed £85 and stood as guarantor on behalf of the Trustees of the chapel. This was a very large sum in those days, possibly a weaver's savings for old age and irreplaceable should he be called upon to honour his bond. Unfortunately, his wife became so upset by this gesture it became the cause of her suicide. For a time in the 1870s the chapel enjoyed a period of prosperity under the patronage of Mr James Moorby, master of the cotton mill at Twiston. Unfortunately, the mill was burnt down and many of the workers moved away to find other employment.

Fig. 17. Martin Top, Salem Congregational Chapel, Rimington, Lancashire.

In 1867 John Laycock came into East Lancashire bringing with him the organ he had built for Martin Top Salem Congregational Chapel, Rimington Lancashire. When it was finally erected the imposing casework became the main feature of the chapel interior. The case facade consists of five 'flats', four having three pipes each and the central one is a pedamented arch holding seven pipes. The instrument is free standing and clothed in a complete pine case framed and panelled. All the pipework is placed upon a common soundboard and unenclosed. Wherever possible a complete casework was provided, not simply a panelled frontal. John Laycock regarded the provision of a case almost as important as tonal quality. At Martin Top the casework appears to contain a much larger instrument, but this is its tonal success; every pipe having room to speak and the casework collecting and dispersing the tone in a similar fashion as the bowl of a violin or cello.

Fig. 18. Martin Top Salem Congregational Chapel, Rimington. Lancashire 1867 John Laycock organ

Martin Top, Salem, Congregational Chapel, Rimington, Lancashire

Specification of 1867 organ built by John Laycock
Manual. CC-g: Pedal CCC-F coupled to manual.

Bourdon	16'
Double Open Diapason	16'
Open Diapason	8'
Stopped Diapason	8'
Dulciana	8'
Principal	4'
Fifteenth	2'

The cost of this instrument was £80 with an additional 10 shilling (50p) for the organ stool. In 1870, tuning this instrument was charged at 8s-6d (42½p) per visit and 2s-6d (12½p) for travelling expenses.

The village of Rimington, Lancashire has close connections with the hymn writer Francis Duckworth, who composed the internationally famous hymn tune named 'Rimington' to words by Isacc Watts 'Jesus Shall Reign' along with several others amongst which are included Stopper Lane, set to the words 'Praise Ye The Lord'. Martin Top 'At Even E're The Sun Was Set' and Colne 'Jesus The Very Thought Of Thee'.[24]

Francis Duckworth was the son of Robert and Mary Ann Duckworth in business as grocers and general dealers at the bottom of Windy Bank and in the Cloth Hall in Colne. The family later moved to Stopper Lane where they took over the post office and grocery shop, this being situated next to the Wesleyan Chapel. The music there was provided by a small orchestra of which Francis' father and three uncles were members. They were an ambitious group of amateurs, who, after working long hours would travel for a few miles to remote farm houses where a weekly rehearsal would be held and a welcome supper follow.[25]

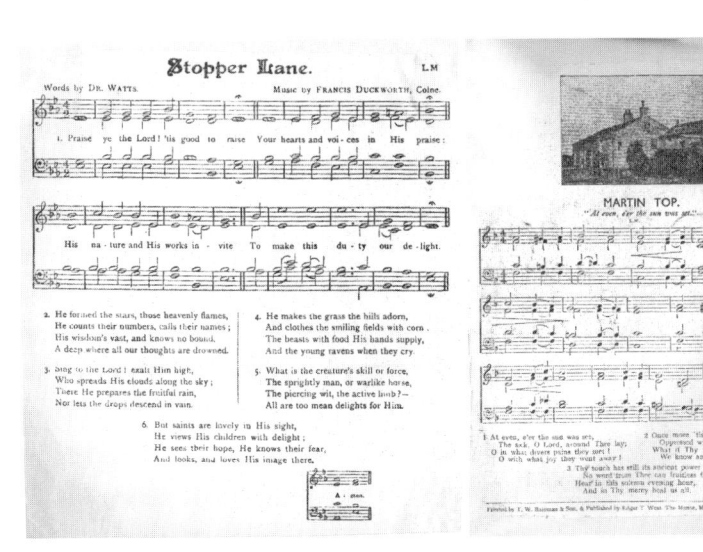

Left; Fig. 19
Right, Fig. 20

Young Francis was given music lessons at an early age which cost ten shillings per quarter (50p). Later he began to play the organ which usurped the chapel band. In later life Francis opened his own grocery business at 33 Market Street, Colne in 1889. It was at this time that he became a member of Albert Road Methodist Church and also the deputy organist, later holding the position of regular organist for forty years.[26]

Francis Duckworth was inspired by the performances of the organist John Henry Jude who drew large crowds to hear his recitals played upon a French mustel reed organ. Some years later a London firm of musical instrument importers advertised a Mustel instrument for sale; Francis Duckworth paid a visit to their showrooms; there he was approached by an assistant wearing a skull cap and frock coat. He informed Francis that he was the owner of a Mustel Reed Organ and of their superior quality of tone.

Francis Duckworth was allowed to play one of their Mustels' and later two gentlemen entered the showroom, one having a foreign accent and later he found himself being introduced to *none other* than Monsieur Mustel himself, who was visiting England for the first time. Francis Duckworth could not believe his luck; to meet the man in whose factory in Paris, the instrument he was about to purchase had been built. Also for whom the composer Alexandre Guilmant had written part music.[27]

Francis Duckworth purchased the Mustel Reed Organ and composed his most inspired hymn tune 'Rimington'. It was first sung at the Colne Whitsun procession in 1904 and claimed to be the most popular hymn tune of the century being included in over thirty English Hymnals and appearing in ten languages.

The tune was reproduced by several recording companies and became extremely popular with the brass band movement. Later it achieved greater fame when it was sung by the Lancashire Fusiliers on Mount Calvary following Lord Allenby's capture of Jerusalem. By 1932, forty-thousand copies of 'Rimington' had been published.[28]

Fig. 21. Francis Duckworth at the Mustel Organ.

Between 1869-79 seven new instruments were produced amongst which were included Christ Church, Colne, Lancashire costing £276-0s-0d this was fitted into the case of a previous organ: Cullingworth Baptist Church, Yorks with 17 stops costing £195-0s-0d. This church has been converted into a dwelling and the instrument purchased by an organ enthusiast in Halifax, where it is to be incorporated into a larger organ for a private residence. The Wesleyan Chapel, Leeds with three manuals and 33 stops costing £392-0s-0d. During this period it is recorded that Charles Bannister became an apprentice aged sixteen years on October 17th, 1875. The business was kept alive with tuning and repairs together with a variety of incidental work. It is also noted that John Laycock was now making coffins for the trade and that their price had also increased. A plain one cost £5-10s-0d and an oak panelled one was a little more expensive at six guineas. The business must have made a steady turnover as it is noted they now had an apprentice, who was the son of John Laycock's foreman Charles Bannister.

The Parish Church of St. Nicholas
Sabden, Pendle, Lancashire

The foundation stone of St. Nicholas' Church was laid on October 23rd, 1838 by the Dowager Mrs. Starkie of Huntroyd Hall. The building was opened for public worship in 1841 by the Revd. Hugh Stowell, Rector of Christ's, Church, Salford, Manchester. Sabden, at that period was in the Parish of Whalley, obtained its individual parish status in 1849; granted by the Bishop of Manchester. Shortly after this event, a taste for church music of a more refined form than had previously been provided by violin and cello, was now desired. A subscription was commenced amongst the members of the congregation for the purpose of raising funds to purchase an organ.

The first instrument to be installed in St. Nicholas's was placed in the small western gallery; it had previously stood in Colne Parish Church. This instrument gave service until 1879-80, when some major refurbishment was carried out to the internal arrangements of the church. This work included the enlargement of the western gallery and the purchase of a new organ built by John Laycock of West Closes, Glusburn.[29]

This instrument was built within a panelled free standing casework of selected pitch pine, the framing finished with turned cappings and the side towers with crown mouldings. The console is of polished mahogany and the sliding doors are arranged to protect both the console and part of the pedalboard. The drawstops are fitted into vertical jambs and their designations are highlighted with flourishes, a style prevalent in John Laycock's work.

The voicing of this instrument has a 'singing' quality associated with the 'old' English organ. There is an abundance of tonal colour between the two departments of Swell and Great, and the full choruses are never taken to the point of 'brashness', or too powerful for the building.

The specification is as follows.
Built by John Laycock of West Closes, Glusburn. Yorks 1879-80
Manuals CC-G. Pedals CCC-E: Mechanical action throughout

Great.	**Swell**	**Pedal**
Open Diapason	Bourdon	Bourdon
Viol di Gamba	Open Diapason	Open Diapason
Claribel	Viol d'Amour	Pedal Octave
Flute (tenor.C.)	Gedact	
Principal	Principal	
Fifteenth	Piccolo	
Sesquialtera	Horn	
Clarinet	Oboe (tenor. C.)	

Couplers
Swell to Great   Swell to Pedal   Great to Pedal
3 combination pedals to Great and Pedal
2 combination pedals to Swell.

This instrument was completely restored without any tonal or mechanical alterations by Messrs. David Wells, Organbuilders of Liverpool, 1995.

Fig. 22. St. Nicholas' Parish Church. Sabden. Pendle. Organ built by John Laycock 1879-80.

In 1880 John Laycock received his most important commission so far; this was to build an instrument for Bolton Abbey, North Yorkshire. The Augustinian Priory was established circa 1150AD. Most of the present structure is now a preserved ruin, the remaining nave and side aisles are now the Parish Church. The old chancel has retained some Norman work but what remains is mostly 14th century architecture. The nave was restored in 1880 by the architect George Edmund Street, who used the Early English style whilst providing a glorious west front.

At the completion of the restoration of the abbey, an organ was in preparation at the 'organ gallery' at West Closes and finally brought to Bolton Abbey, Yorks by horse drawn conveyance and erected at the east end of the north aisle. Again there is a complete casework, which was so important to John Laycock; it is panelled to impost level with a framework above to support the facade pipework. The instrument has three manuals and twenty-nine speaking stops and cost £500. The casework and organ stool an extra £66. The original specification as John Laycock left it is given.

Manuals CC-A 58 notes: Pedal CCC-F 30 notes

Great
Bourdon	16' wood
Open Diapason	8' metal
Clarabella	8' metal
Harmonic Flute	4' metal
Principal	4' metal
Twelfth	$2^{2/3}$' metal
Fifteenth	2' metal
Mixture	3rks metal
Trumpet	8' metal

Pedal
Open Diapason	16' wood
Bourdon	16' wood
Principal	8' wood
Bass Flute	8' wood
Saube Flute	4' metal
Clarionet	8' metal

Swell
Lieblich Bourdon	16' wood
Open Diapason	8' metal
Salicional	8' metal
Voix Celeste	8' metal
Lieblich Gedackt	8' metal
Octave	4' metal
Piccolo	2' metal
Mixture	3rks metal
Horn	8' metal
Oboe	8' metal
Tremulant	

Choir
Dulciana	8' metal
Viol d'Gamba	8' metal
Lieblich Gedackt	8' wood

Couplers
Swell to Great   Great to Pedal
Swell to Choir   Choir to Pedal
Swell to Pedal Swell to Great Super Octave
3 Combination pedals to Great and Pedal
3 Combination pedals to Swell

This instrument was originally blown by a Kinetic hydraulic engine, the water was drawn from the River Wharfe which flows below the Abbey grounds.

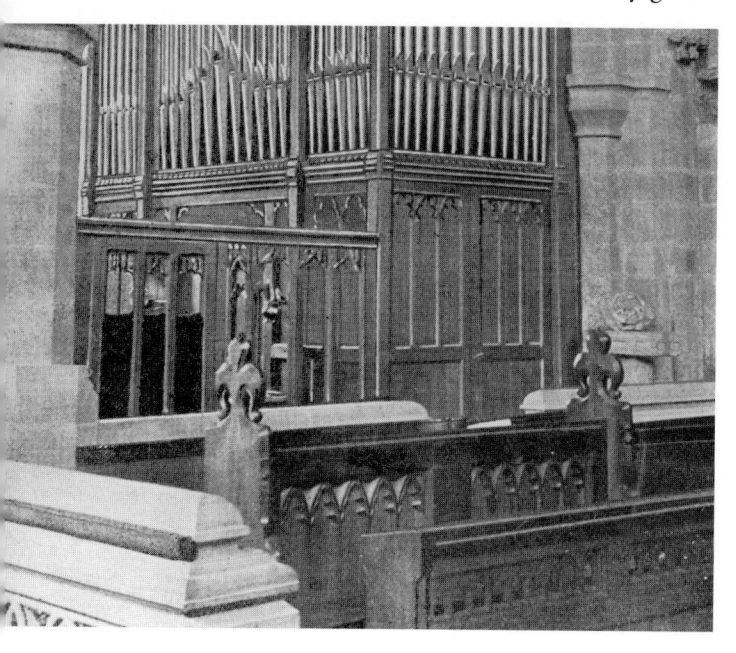

Fig. 23. Bolton Abbey, West Yorkshire. Organ built by John Laycock of West Closes, Glusburn 1880.

Photo. B. Hughes

In the construction of his instruments John Laycock never sacrificed purity and sweetness of tone in order to produce a loud and ponderous organ. He used the best of materials available, he was particularly insistent on the supply of well seasoned timber; good quality leather and stout metal in the pipe work.

All manuals had ivory covered keys, mahogany was used for the soundboards and selected hard and softwood for the wooden pipes. The cabinet work of his organ cases was of a high order, correctly jointed and robustly constructed with much thought being given to correct proportions. Wherever possible a complete case was provided, panelled on three sides with the front elevation containing an attached drawstop console, panelled on either side, above which was a pipe display of either plain or decorated pipework.

Amongst the old shop books was discovered an Inventory & Valuation Book of the workshop at West Closes, Glusburn, Yorks. It appears to be a 'home made' note book possibly made by John himself; the corners of the covers are picked out with floral motifs and the edges coloured in a 'tile' effect. The book is dated 1885 Inventory & Valuation Book 1885: Payments, Wages, Materials etc.[30]

Windmill Lathes	£150		Tenon Saws	6s-0d	(30p)
Boring Machine	£5		Dovetail Saws	3s-0d	(15p)
Mortice Machine	£5		Trenching Plane	6s-0d	(30p)
Benches	£5		Plough Plane	15s-0d	(75p)
Plane Irons	£1-7s-0d	(£1.35p)	Mould Planes	£1-6s-0d	(£1.30p)
Trying Plane	15s-0d	(75p)	Punches	10s-0d	(50p)
Jack Plane	10s-0d	(50p)	Saw sets	4s-0d	(20p)
Hand Saws	8s-0d	(40p)	Beam Compass	2s-0d	(10p)

Several of these entries are of interest and lend credibility to some of the stories centred around this remarkable figure John Laycock. Perhaps the most significant entries are those which refer to Windmill Lathes: Repairs to Windmill: and the names of the suppliers for organ parts. Mr. Shield for organ pipes: Alexander Young, organbuilder of Manchester and Alfred Palmer. The foregoing firms supplied John Laycock with items that his early workshop was not equipped to produce.

1889, Payment For Materials (Shop books).[31]

Stop Knobs to R. Foster	£1-10s-0d	(150p)
Keyboards	£3-12s-7d	(£3.63$^{1}/_{2}$)
Blacklead	4$^{1}/_{2}$d	(5p)
Varnish & Stain	11d	(5$^{1}/_{2}$p)
Mr, Shield for organ pipes	£10-0s-0d	
Paul Pearson for repairs to Windmill	£4-6s-0d	(£4.30p)
Business Cards	7s-6d	(37$^{1}/_{2}$p)
Alexander Young. Organbuilder Manchester	19s-0d	(90p)
Alfred Palmer. Organ Pipes	£12-3s-7d	(£12.18$^{1}/_{2}$)

Between 1880-89 ten new organs were built, these included St. Leonard's Parish Church, Langho, Clitheroe, Lancashire (1882). Saltley Road Chapel, Birmingham (1883). Cowling Parish Church. North Yorks (1883). Moor Lane, Methodist Chapel, Clitheroe, Lancashire (1888). The Wesleyan Chapel, Steeton. North Yorks (1889). St. John's Parish Church. Cononly, North Yorks (1890).[32]

St. Leonard's Parish Church
Langho, Clitheroe, Lancashire

This building replaced an older church which is still extant and under the Council For The Care Of Churches. The present church of St. Leonard's was built in 1880 in the Early English style. The external walling is of random cut stone supported by buttressing having plain cappings. The internal arrangements are of nave with five bays, side aisles and a large chancel. All the woodwork is carried out in English oak.

The instrument in St. Leonard's is the work of John Laycock of West Closes, Glusburn, North Yorks. The casework and console is positioned behind the choir stalls on the south side of the chancel. Built in 1882, it displays one of Laycock's more mature examples in chorus building. Here the major diapason chorus on the Great or main organ at 8ft - 4ft - 2ft pitches is rich and full and the little flute chorus at 8ft and 4ft has a full round smooth quality. The secondary chorus on the Swell organ has a rich clarity with a full reedy sound, made possible by the introduction of the Sesquialtera Mixture 17:19:22 and topped by a beautifully voiced Orchestral Oboe. The casework is of English oak and the facade pipework is of heavy spotted metal. On the west side of the casework is to be found a rank of non-speaking wooden pipes made to correct scaling- with properly formed mouths. The bodies of these pipes are really oak facings of thick sections of oak boards, quarter sawn to reveal the 'silver grain'. No expense was spared at the time when this instrument was built; the total cost being £235 and the organ stool £12.

The mechanical action is rather heavy, a common characteristic associated with the Laycock style of actions, however, everything is robustly constructed from the best of materials and the drawstop heads are highlighted with flourishes in the Laycock style. The specification has remained unaltered to the present time.

Built by John Laycock. West Closes, Glusburn. Yorks 1882.
Manual CC-G: Pedal CCC-F

Great		**Swell**		**Pedal**	
Open Diapason	8'	Double Diapason	16'	Bourdon	16'
Clarabella	8'	Open Diapason	8'	Open Diapason	16'
Flute	4'	Salicional	8'	Couplers	
Principal	4'	Stopped Diapason	8'	Swell to Great	
Twelfth	2 2/3	Principal	4'	Great to Pedal	
Fifteenth	2'	Piccolo	2'	Swell to Pedal	
		Sesquialtera	3rks		
		Oboe	8'		

2 combination pedals to Great & Pedal 2 combination pedals to Swell
This instrument was restored in 1973

Fig. 24. The Parish Church of St. Leonard's, Langho, Clitheroe, Lancashire.

Left, Fig. 25 St. Leonard's Church. Langho,
Engraved stopheads in Laycock's style.

The opening recital was given by John Turner on September 23rd, 1882.

Programme

Barcarole	Bennet
Offertoire	Salome
Grand Chorus	Salome
Adagio (First Symphony)	Haydn
March from 'Athalia'	Mendelssohn
Largetto (Quartet in B flat)	Mozart
Andante	Batiste
Grand Chorus	Salome (encore).

Below, Fig. 26. John Laycock's trade plate. St. Leonard's Church, Langho, Clitheroe, Lancs.

Fig. 27. 'St. Leonard's Parish Church, Langho, Clitheroe, Lancs. Organ by John Laycock. 1882.

Cowling United Free Chapel
Ickornshaw, North Yorkshire

In 1884 John Laycock returned to Ickornshaw Chapel, West Yorkshire where in 1839 he had purchased from the trustees their old organ for £5. This had been the start of his career into organ building. Now, forty-five years later he returned to build a new organ for the chapel. Here he provided an instrument of two manuals and pedals within a divided casework; the drawstop console was detached and positioned centrally in the choir gallery. The action of this instrument was Laycocks 'pressure' pneumatic. The wind supply was provided by a hydraulic engine with a differential crank fitted to the feeders. The water was pumped from the beck which ran close by the chapel and fed into a storage tank. There were of course occasional problems when during one very dry Springtime and an important weekend occasion, the preacher arriving on horseback on the Saturday evening was pleased to witness the devotion of several members of the congregation who were kneeling beside the beck. 'Whats all this?' he asked. The reply came 'Oh, don't upset yourself, minister; we're only prayin for rain'. The specification and opening recital is given as follows.

Built by John Laycock. 1884.
Manuals CC-A. Pedal CCC-F

Great		**Swell**		**Pedal**	
Open Diapason	8'	Open Diapason	8'	Open Diapason	16'
Dulciana	8'	Salicional	8'	Bourdon	16'
Hohl Flute	8'	Voix Celeste	8'	Bass Flute	8'
Harmonic Flute	4'	Lieblich Gedact	8'		
Principal	4'	Gemshorn	4'		
Fifteenth	2'	Cornopean	8'		
		Oboe	8'		

Couplers
Swell to Great: Swell Super Octave: Swell Sub Octave. Swell to Pedal: Great to Pedal.
2 double acting thumb pistons to Swell. 2 double acting combination pedals to Great and Pedal. Double acting thumb piston to Tremulant.

The opening programme was given on April 12th. 1884 by Dr. William Spark organist of Leeds Town Hall, Yorkshire.

Programme

Concerto in G minor	GF Handel
Andante in A Flat	Batiste
Extemporanesis introduction	
Grand Fugue	J.S. Bach
Quis est Homo, (Stabat Mater)	Rossini
Allegro in B Flat Major	Lemmens
Vesper Hymn, Variations & Fugue	Spark
Andante in C Major	Mendelssohn
Grand Chorus, Hallelujah to the Father	L van Beethoven

Cowling Chapel, West Yorkshire closed for public worship many years ago. The building still stands in the centre of the village a reminder of past glories. The organ was sold and restored and re-erected in St. Vincent's Catholic Church, Hull.

The workshop at West Closes, Glusburn or as it was known locally as the 'organ gallery' was by this time firmly established. John Laycock had acquired a reputation for good reliable and tonally artistic work. He had established a tuning and maintenance service over a wide area; and which was more than competitive alongside contemporary organbuilders.

A selection of costs for tuning and maintenance in Laycock's time is of interest as a comparison of single items then and now.

Fig. 28. Cowling United Free Chapel, Ickornshaw, North Yorks

Shop Book entries: John Laycock. [33]

1867	Clitheroe, Lancashire St. James' Parish Church. Tuning & Travelling expenses from Crosshills. £1-0s-0 (100p)
1869	Colne. Laneshaw Bridge Chapel, Lancashire. Tuning organ & Travelling expenses from Crosshills. £1-0s-0 (100p)
1870	Rimington, Lancashire. Martin Top Chapel. Organ tuning & Expenses. 10/– (50p)
1871	Providing new Tremulant stop. £1-5s-0d (125p)
1873	Mr. Sayer of Colne. Lancashire Tuning organ & travelling expenses from Crosshills. 12/– (60p)
1873	New Dulciana rank 56 pipes metal.£7-10s. (£7.50p)
1879	New stopped pipes CC-g. 10/– (50p)
1883	Organ stools Pine. 10/– (50p) Oak £12-0-0
1888	Haworth. Yorks. Hall Green Chapel.Tuning organ. 2s-6d (12$^{1}/_{2}$p)

John Laycock continued to work in his chosen craft almost to the end of his life. When his health began to fail, he confined himself to the workshop, allowing the younger members of the staff to carry out the erecting of the instruments on site. In spite of the closure of many ecclesiastical buildings, it has been possible to account for thirty new instruments and forty-two restorations in which John Laycock was personally involved. The last instrument to come under his personal supervision was built for Moor Lane Wesleyan Church. Clitheroe. Lancashire in 1888.

This church is built in the Early English style and in more recent times has undergone some modernisation. The external stonework is of particular interest, inspection revealing an abundance of fossil formations on the surfaces of the stone blocks. Internally the building is light and spacious. The organ built by John Laycock is positioned in the choir gallery. The instrument is free standing in a complete pine casework, panelled and painted in artificial wood grain. The console is made of mahogany with vertical drawstop jambs and a straight and parallel pedalboard.

Time has not dealt sympathetically with this instrument which has been out of commission for some years. The quality of the workmanship is all that one expects from John Laycock and the specification is given as follows.

Built by John Laycock of West Closes, Glusburn, Yorks 1888. Cost £500.
Manuals CC-G: Pedals CCC-F. Mechanical action.

Great		Swell		Pedal	
Open Diapason	8'	Open Diapason	8'	Soft Bass	16'
Dulciana	8'	Keraulophon	8'	Bourdon	16'
Stopped Diapason	8'	Vox Angelica	8'		
Gedact	8'	Vox Celeste	8'		
Principal	4'	Octave	4'		
Hohl Flute	4'	Fifteenth	2'		
Harmonic Flute	4'	Oboe	8'		
		Cornopean	8'		
		Tremulant			

Couplers
2 combination pedals to Great & Pedal   Swell to Great
Great to Pedal (duplicated)
2 combination pedals to Swell   Swell to Pedal

John Laycock died on September 13th, 1889 after a short illness hastened by a paralytic stroke. Craven Herald. September, 1889 (sic).[34]

"On Tuesday September 17th, 1889 were laid to rest in the churchyard at Kildwick the remains of John Laycock of West Closes, Glusburn in the Parish of Kildwick, North Yorkshire. As the procession entered the church led by the Revd. A.D.C. Thompson. Vicar of Kildwick, the organist Charles Green of Sutton Church played the 'Dead March in Saul'." As a mark of respect

48 John Laycock

JOHN LAYCOCK 1808-1889

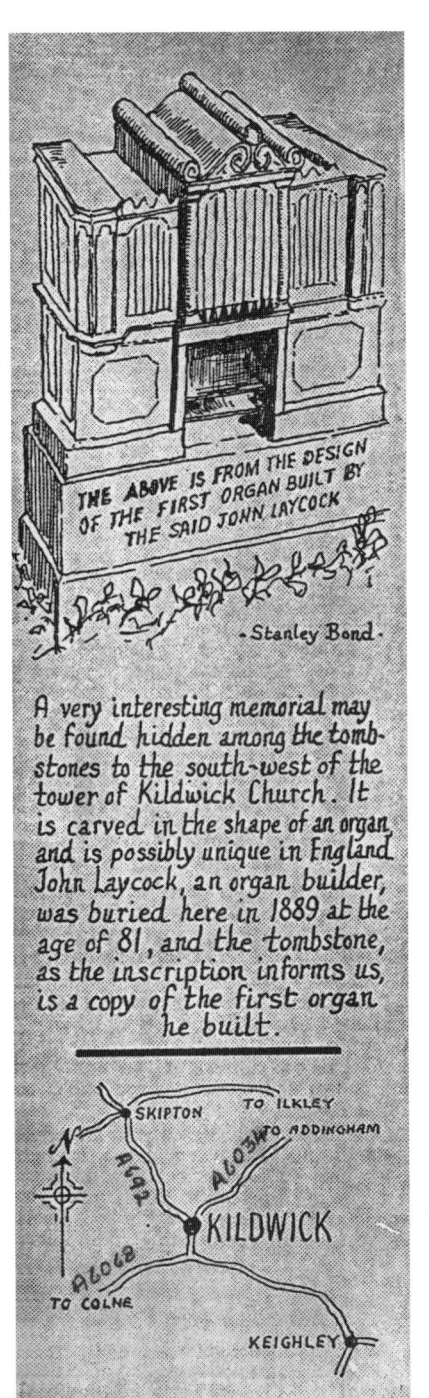

the Vicar of Kildwick had arranged that all the choristers should attend the service. The family of Laycock is, perhaps the oldest residential family in the parish, and there were Laycocks as churchwardens in 1671. The affection and esteem in which the deceased was held was shown by the numbers who attended the church from miles around the district as well as from the immediate neighbourhood. A tribute was paid to John Laycock during the service, referring to his enthusiasm and unbounding search for knowledge even to the end of his days. His accurate memory and pleasant style of imparting knowledge was unique and made him equally welcome amongst young and old. His musical gifts and his taste for fine arts had a stimulating influence amongst his many friends. He received numerous unsolicited testimonials from professional musicians, who were generous with their encouragement in what he was seeking to achieve.

As the cortege left the church the organist played 'O Rest In The Lord' ("Elijah"). The coffin was of polished oak with brass fittings. The pallbearers were Charles Bannister (Shop Foreman); and members of the staff Messrs. Robert Thompson. William Whittaker. Sidney Stow, William Dawson, and Thomas Bottomley.

The organ building business of John Laycock is to be continued by his son William and foreman Charles Bannister; and will trade under the name of Laycock and Bannister.

THE ABOVE IS FROM THE DESIGN OF THE FIRST ORGAN BUILT BY THE SAID JOHN LAYCOCK

- Stanley Bond -

A very interesting memorial may be found hidden among the tombstones to the south-west of the tower of Kildwick Church. It is carved in the shape of an organ and is possibly unique in England. John Laycock, an organ builder, was buried here in 1889 at the age of 81, and the tombstone, as the inscription informs us, is a copy of the first organ he built.

Left, Fig. 30.

Left, Fig. 29. The grave of John Laycock. Kildwick Churchyard, North Yorkshire.

Chapters 2 John Laycock
References
1. *The Craven Herald. September 1889*
2. *Ibid*
3. *Ibid*
4. *Census Records 1841. Leeds Central Library*
5. *Ibid*
6. *Craven Herald. September 1889*
7. *Wm Neville Blakey. Archive Collection*
8. *Ibid*
9. *Ibid*
10. *Mr John Laycock. Thomas H. Haswell. Keighley (Booklet)*
11. *Wm Neville Blakey. Archive Collection*
12. *Ibid*
13. *Ibid*
14. *Ibid*
15. *Ibid*
16. *Mr. John Laycock. Thomas H Haswell. Keighley. (Booklet)*
17. *Ibid*
18. *St. Peter's . Leeds. John Busby. 1896*
19. *Colne Parish Church. James Robert MacVicar. Coulton & Co Ltd. 1949*
20. *Ibid*
21. *History & Associations of Altham & Huncoat. Robert Ainsworth*
22. *Ibid*
23. *Wm Neville Blakey. Archive Collection*
24. *Francis. Duckworth – 'A Business Man's Hobby'. Coulton & Co. Colne 1936*
25. *Ibid*
26. *Ibid*
27. *Ibid*
28. *Ibid*
29. *Birth Of A Village. Charles Moorhouse*
30. *Wm Neville Blakey. Archive Collection*
31. *Ibid*
32. *Laycock & Bannister. Catalogue*
33. *Wm Neville Blakey. Archive Collection*
34. *The Craven Herald. December 1889*

CHAPTER THREE

Laycock & Bannister

ORGANBUILDERS. CROSSHILLS. YORKSHIRE

AFTER THE DEATH OF JOHN LAYCOCK IN 1889 THE BUSINESS AT WEST CLOSES, GLUSBURN was continued by his son, William, who took into partnership his father's foreman Charles Bannister. The firm now traded under the title of Laycock & Bannister.

In the census returns of 1881, the Bannister family who were to play such an important role in the development of this organ building firm; are recorded as living in close proximity to the Laycock's. The organ building members of the Bannister family are given below:

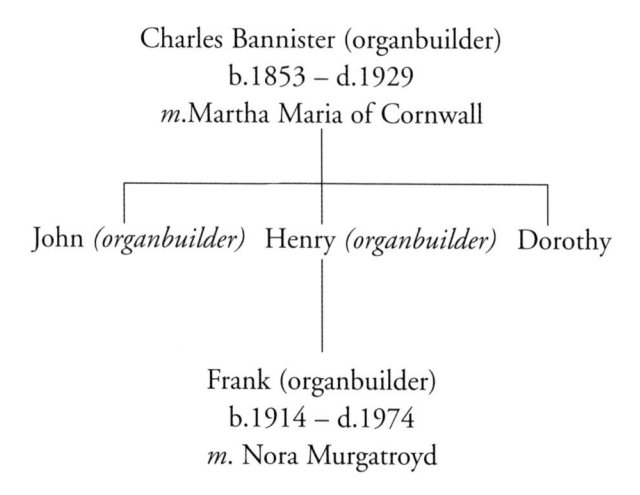

Charles Bannister (organbuilder)
b.1853 – d.1929
*m.*Martha Maria of Cornwall

John *(organbuilder)*   Henry *(organbuilder)*   Dorothy

Frank (organbuilder)
b.1914 – d.1974
m. Nora Murgatroyd

The census of 1881 records the Bannister household living at Greenfield Place, Glusburn, near Crosshills. Yorks.[1]

Census. 1881
Charles Bannister (organ building journeyman) *Aged 28*
Martha Maria Bannister. Wife Cornwall
Martha Binns Servant *Aged 56*
James Smith (Worsted Wool Sorter) *Aged 27*
Sarah Smith Wife *Aged 28*
John Smith Son *Aged 3*
Mary Elizabeth Daughter *Aged 11 months.*

The new partnership appeared to be a successful one and to progress with the same zeal and enthusiasm as exhibited by the founder himself. Between 1889-1893, the first three years of the new partnership saw a steady flow of commissions, a wide tuning area had been built up and repair work came in on a regular basis. Over this short period thirteen new instruments had been built for[2]

1889	Steeton Wesleyan Chapel, North Yorks: 2 manuals. Cost £315	
1889	Hawksbridge, Baptist Chapel, West Yorks: 2 manuals. Cost £154. Stool 10/–	
1890	Nelson. Lancashire, Independent Methodist Chapel. 2 manuals. Cost £216	
1891	Cononley, North Yorks, St. John's Parish Church. 2 manuals. Cost £145	
1891	Whalley, Lancashire, Wesleyan Chapel. 2 manuals. Cost £164. Stool 10/–	
1892	Sawood, Wesleyan Chapel, West Yorks. 2 manuals. Cost £104. Stool 10/–	
1892	Burnley, St. Stephen's Parish Church. 2 manuals. Cost £380. Stool 12/–	
1893	Bradford, West Yorks, Denholme, Wesleyan Chapel. 2 manuals. Cost £180	
1893	Lancashire, Colne, Primet Bridge Free Chapel, 2 manuals. Cost £200	
1893	Lancashire, Nelson, Salem Chapel. 2 manuals. Cost £230. Tuning £5	
1894	Blackburn, Sabden Wesleyan Chapel. 2 manuals	
1894	Long Preston, North Yorks, Wesleyan Chapel. 2 manuals. Cost £210	
1894	Greengates, North Yorks, St. John's Church. 2 manuals. Cost £300 Oak casework £27; Brass plaque £1-15s-0d	

By 1890, Messrs. Laycock & Bannister were advertising in musical trade journals, and the instrument built for Steeton Wesleyan Chapel appears in *Musical Opinion* for December 1890.

Built by Laycock & Bannister. West Closes. Glusburn. 1890.

Great		Swell		Pedal	
Double Open Diapason	16'	Open Diapason	8'	Grand Bourdon	16'
Open Diapason	8'	Salicional	8'	Open Diapason	16'
Dulciana	8'	Voix Celeste	8'		
Hohl Flute	8'	Lieblich Gedact	8'		
Flute Harmonic	4'	Octave	4'		
Principal	4'	Oboe	8'		
Fifteenth	2'	Tremulant			
Clarionet	8'				

3 combination pedals to Great & Pedal
3 combination pedals to Swell
Mechanical action throughout.

The opening recital was given by Charles Ernest Melville. FRCO, on August 30th, 1890.

Programme

Prelude & Fugue in G minor	J.S. Bach
La Servaenata	Braga
Fantasia on Jerusalem The Golden	
Chorus of Angels	Scotson Clarke
Fixed In His Everlasting Seat	GF Handel

 Now with an increase in new commissions, rebuilding of existing instruments and tuning and maintenance contracts, it became necessary to acquire larger and better equipped premises. A site suitable for development was purchased in Aire Street, Crosshills, North Yorks. Here a purpose built workshop was erected and completed in 1893. The Laycock & Bannister shop books describe the new building as laid out in three sections and designated workshops Nos 1, 2 and 3. Number 1. workshop was on the top floor and used as a store for timber and wooden pipes which were made on the premises. The species of timber kept in stock was itemised e.g sections of second and best pine; Redwood; Cedar; White Deal; Teak; Mahogany; Pitch Pine: Wainscott Oak; Danzig Oak; Canary Wood. Included too, were-sets of pedalboards; tremulants; stopped bass pipes; Dulciana bass octaves; Violin bass octaves; bass flutes; harmonic flutes and gedacts; swell bourdons and sliders.

 Number 2 workshop contained circular saws, boring, morticing and screwing machines, skins for bellows and pallets, pitch pine pillars, saws and moulding planes, work benches, sharpening equipment for saws; storage for mechanical actions, roller-boards and springs, soundboards, slides and manual coupling blocks.

 Number 3 workshop was on the ground floor. Here was positioned the gas engine which drove the woodworking machinery on a line shaft system. On this floor soundboards and pneumatic actions were produced, there was adequate space for the erection and assembling of instruments; and a room was set aside equipped with a voicing machine; this was made from a keyboard and a windchest from a disused organ. Here a workbench was provided, with a set of mandrils for use in shaping the metal pipes and, away from the general noise of the workshop, a craftsman with a knowledge of voicing was involved in shaping the pipe mouths and lips in order to introduce the tonal colours into the organ. Nearby was the paint shop stocked with stains, oils, varnishes, paint, naptha and dyes. There were also two external storage sheds for Laycock & Bannister, carried a large selection of timbers and additional storage was necessary. In this area was stored Japanese Oak, Pencil Cedar: Floorboards; Odessa Oak; plywood and packing cases. The building at Aire Street, Crosshills was a very complete and well equipped workshop and covered an area of 1,185 sq yards, and carried a staff of fourteen. Laycock & Bannister Shop Books: Cost of building work for new organ works 1893.[3]

Land	£129-16s-0d
Joiners work	£110-0s-0d
Davy Smith Jointing Co.	£6-13s-2d
Masonwork	£269-12s-7½d
William Smith: Slating.	£35-0s 0d
G. Greenwood. Ironmongery.	£5-0s-0d
Jas, Shepley. Glazier.	£14-0s-0d
J. Wilson. Gas Fitter.	£15-19s-0d
H.J. Riddiough. Timber.	£11-14s-0d
Spenser Clark for Deeds	£4-5s-0d
F. Greenwood. Ashes	£1-2s-0d
Harrison Greenwood. Painting	£5-2s-0d
Sewerage Co.	£2-15s-0d
New End Room	£110-12s-6d
	£721-11s-3½d

Fig. 31. Messrs. Laycock & Bannister Organbuilders. Aire Street, Crosshills. North Yorks.

In the first decade of the new workshop twenty-three new instruments can be accounted for together with seven complete restorations. The number of tuning and maintenance contracts had increased and there was a steady flow of minor repairs which provided for a busy workshop. Amongst the instruments built over this period were included.[4]

1897 Bradford, West Yorks. Egypt, Methodist Free Chapel. Cost £350. (Now in the Catholic Church Millom, South Lake-Districts)

1897 Nelson, Lancs, Cooper Street, Wesleyan Chapel

1898 Clitheroe, Lancs, Waddington, Wesleyan Chapel. 2 manuals. Cost £150

1898 Staffordshire, Tunstall. Primitive Methodist Chapel. 3 manuals. (Cost £450. Hydraulic engine £52.)

1898	Shipley, West Yorks, Tong Park, Wesleyan Chapel. 2 manuals. Cost £375. (Organ Stool £12)
1899	Nelson, Lancs, Briercliffe Methodist, Elim Chapel. 2 manuals Cost £375. (Organ Stool £12. Tuning £3-12s-0d)
1900	Burnley, Lancs, Zion Chapel. 2 manuals. Cost £275
1900	Masham, North Yorks, Wesleyan Chapel. 2 manuals
1901	Colne, Lancs. Kelbrook, St. Mary's Parish Church. 2 manuals. Cost £238. (Plaque £1-15s-0d. Tuning £2)
1901	Burnley, Lancs. St. Catherine's Parish Church. 3 manuals. Cost £535. (Extra for design of casework £6. Tuning £5.)
1901	Oxenhope, West Yorks. Thornton Parish Church. 3 manuals. Cost £550. (casework and pipe decoration £20)
1901	Burnley, Lancs. Hollingreave Congregational. 2 manuals
1902	Barnoldswick, West Yorks. Bethesda Baptist Chapel. 3 manuals. Cost £320
1903	Burnley, Lancs. Ebenezer Baptist Chapel. 3 manuals
1903	Colne, Lancs. Trawden. Methodist Chapel. 2 manuals
1904	Bradford, West Yorks. Wilsden Congregational Chapel. 3 manuals
1904	Haworth, West Yorks. Wesleyan Chapel. 3 manuals. Cost £ 480

In the firm's shop books (1889-1895) are recorded the wages of several of the staff. It is interesting too, that the firm retained some rural traditions after their move into the township of Crosshills – an entry begins 'Cock to run with hens, three shillings and sixpence'. Perhaps at this period the firm sold eggs cheaply to their employees.

Laycock & Bannister Shop Books 1889.[5]

1889	William Henry Laycock, apprentice 1st. year 3s-6d weekly. (nephew)
1891	William Laycock (senior) £5-12s-0d (£5.60p)
1891	Charles Bannister. £5-12s-0d (£5.60p)
1891	William Whittaker. £4-17s-0d (£4.85p)
1891	Richard Thompson. £4-18s-3d (£4.90p)
1891	William Henry Barry, apprentice 1st year 3s-6d weekly (17$^1/_2$p)
1893	William Brierley, commenced apprenticeship 3s-6d per week. Jan 5th to be raised on his birthday December 27th. 1893.
1893	John Sampson. £1-5s-0d per week. (£1.25p)
1894	J.H.Laycock, commenced apprenticeship aged 15 years, 3s-6d weekly raised yearly by one shilling. (5p)
1895	W.R. Thompson. £5-10s-0d. (£5.50p)
1895	W. Berry. £2-2s-1d. (£2.11p)
1896	Cock to run with hens. 3s-6d (17$^1/_2$p).

Weaver and Organ Builder

St. Catherine's Parish Church
Burnley, Lancs

St. Catherine's is a large lofty building erected in 1897 in the, 'Gothic' style. The front elevation is stone cladded with side and end sections of brickwork. Internally the walling throughout is of Accrington facing bricks. The nave is long, terminating in a very wide chancel at the crossing. On the south side is a large ante-chapel the east end being finished in an octagonal apse. The close boarded roof is supported by large ribbed trusses resting on stone templates at window-sill level, this necessitating the use of massive curved wooden arches. At the west end is a large spacious gallery.

The organ built by Messrs Laycock & Bannister of Crosshills, Yorks is positioned at the east end of the north aisle, a parclose screen separates it from the choir. The casework is of selected pitch pine stained to match the internal woodwork within the church. It is panelled up to impost level, above which the facade pipework forming the Open Diapason on the Great organ is of spotted metal pipework with French mouths.

The casework is of triangular form and divided into five flats finished with heavy pipe shades. The drawstop console is positioned centrally within the casework.

St. Catherine's Parish Church, Burnley. Messrs. Laycock & Bannister. 1901.

Great CC-A		Swell		Choir	
Bourdon	16'	Bourdon	16'	Dulciana	8'
Large Open Diapason	8'	Open Diapason	8'	Lieblich Gedact	8'
Small Open Diapason	8'	Rohr Flute	8'	Saube Flute	4'
Hohl Flute	8'	Viol D'Orchestra	8'	Clarinet	8'
Harmonic Flute	4'	Vox Angelica	8'		
Principal	4'	Viola	4'	**Couplers**	
Mixture	3rks	Piccolo	2'		
Trumpet	8'	Cornopean	8'	Swell to Great	
		Oboe	8'	Swell to Pedal	
Pedal. CCC-F		Tremulant		Swell to Choir	
				Swell Super Octave	
Bourdon	16'				
Open Diapason	16'	Great to Pedal			
Bass Flute	8'	Choir to Pedal			

3 combination pedals to Great & Pedal: 3 combination pedals to Swell
Mechanical action to manuals: Pneumatic action to Pedals

Scartop Sunday School, Stanbury
Haworth West, Yorks

This Sunday School was founded in 1818 in the reign of George III. The building was managed by the Wesleyan denomination and there was evidently much support for the work carried out. In 1869 a complete rebuilding took place, the outcome of which was a school and chapel. The teaching was undenominational, but nevertheless firmly entrenched in Wesleyan traditions. The school catered for 32 girls and 33 boys and lessons were given in reading, spelling, religion and singing.

In 1878 there is a record for the purchase of two dozen spelling books; there was also a well stocked library and the registers are available from 1898. There are also several records of chapel trips organised by the Trustees, these being made by horses and wagonettes.

The Scartop Charity (an old term for Sunday School Anniversary) is still held on the second Sunday in June. This event dates back to the very early days of the school and is held in the open air, away from the chapel on land near Ponden Mill. In the early days the Heatons of Ponden Hall owned the Ponden Corn Mill and were members of Scartop Chapel. Mr. John Heaton was a musician and composed an anthem – 'Show Me Thy Ways O Lord", a vocal score for choir and organ. This event was very popular and the speakers attracted congregations of some 3,000 people to the open air event. The music was provided by a choir and an orchestra consisting of violins, cornets, clarinet, trombones, piccolo, double bass and harmonium. On several occasions the Haworth Brass Band took part.[6]

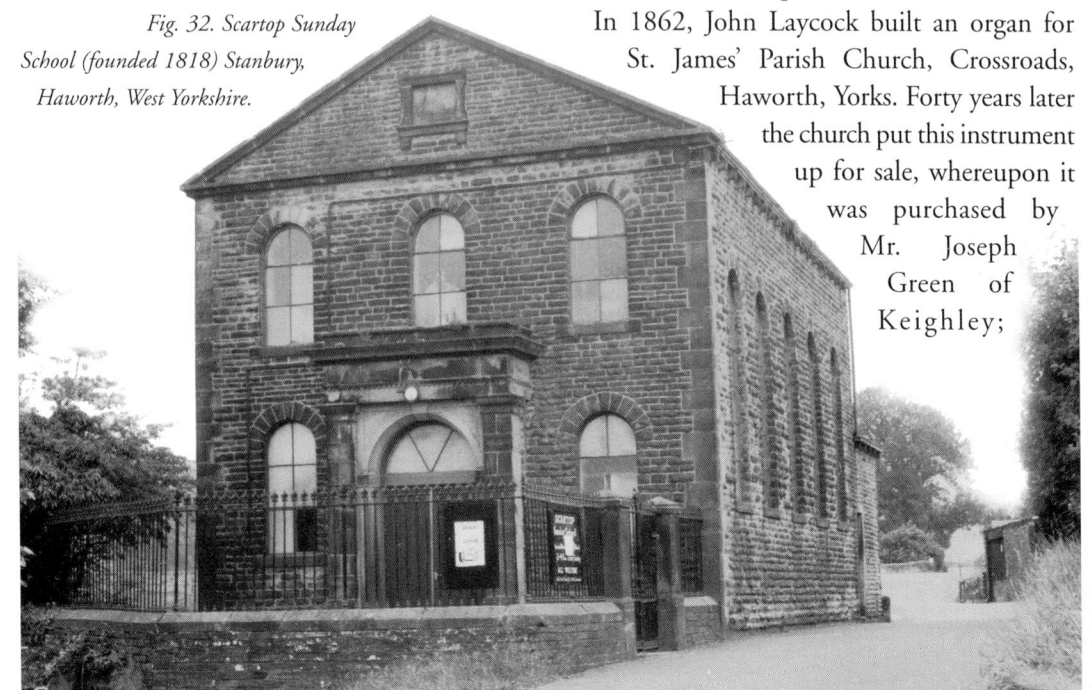

In 1862, John Laycock built an organ for St. James' Parish Church, Crossroads, Haworth, Yorks. Forty years later the church put this instrument up for sale, whereupon it was purchased by Mr. Joseph Green of Keighley;

Fig. 32. Scartop Sunday School (founded 1818) Stanbury, Haworth, West Yorkshire.

Photo. B. Hughes

Fig. 33. Scartop Sunday School: Chamber Organ built by John Laycock, West Closes, Glusburn, Yorks. 1862.

who presented it to Scartop Sunday School in memory of his parents. Built by John Laycock of West Closes, Glusburn, Yorkshire, 1862. Scartop 1905.

Manual. CC-F. 54 notes. Pedal. CCC-D. 27 notes.	
R.H. stop jamb.	L.H. stop jamb
Open Diapason	Stopped Diapason T.C.
Dulciana	Principal
Pedal Coupler	Fifteenth
Bourdon	

The pipework is on a single soundboard with a separate chest for the Pedal Bourdon. The casework is panelled and free standing with a non speaking facade of gilded pipes. The voicing is mild and of a pure clear tone which admirably suits the building in which the instrument stands where it is positioned to the rear of the choir gallery.

In 1924 a new piano was purchased costing £48 and at a meeting it was decided the 'Amen' would be sung at the end of every hymn.

In 1934, electricity had been supplied to the Stanbury Co-Operative stores and later to Ponden Mill in 1937, Scartop Chapel being supplied in 1945. Up to this time the organ was blown by a hand mechanism which has been retained, In 1960 an electrical fan blower provided wind for the organ.

From 1904, at the end of the first decade of the Aire Street workshop and the closing years of the 1914-18 war, twenty-four new instruments had been completed. The area of work now covered north and west Yorkshire; Manchester; Staffordshire and Wigan. There was too, a continual full order book of tuning and maintenance and other repair work. As the war years continued, so work of this type became of less importance and members of the organ building staff were called into the armed forces. It is noticeable too, that the firm still continued with the local undertaking side of the business until well into the 1900s.

Laycock's Shop Books 1919[7]
R.H. Greenwood of Crosshills.

To one best wainscott oak coffin	£9-3s-8d
To brass furniture and engraved plate	£2-11s-6d
To best cashmere shawl, wadding & lining	£1-6s-6d
To polishing & fuming	12s-0d
To one hearse and five cabs	£3-12s-0d
To attendance at funeral	8s-0d
To six notices	6s-0d
	£17-19s-8d

The instruments completed during these difficult years which included those of the Great War 1914-18 included the following:[8]

1905	Colne, Lancs, Laneshaw Bridge, Wesleyan Chapel. 2 manuals. Cost. £234. Tuning 18s-4d. (93p)
1905	Wigan, Lancs, Primitive Methodist Chapel, Aspull. 2 manuals
1906	Burnley, Lancs, Wheatley Lane, Wesleyan Chapel. 2 manuals
1906	Ripon, North Yorks, Bishop Monkton, Parish Church. 2 manuals
1907	Colne, Lancs, Foulridge Parish Church, St. Michaels. 2 Manuals Cost. £400
1908	Farnhill, West Yorks, Primitive Methodist Chapel. 2 manuals
1908	Haworth, West Yorks, Mill Hey Primitive Methodist Chapel. 2 manuals
1909	Clitheroe, Lancs, Low Moor, U.R. Chapel. 2 manuals
1909	Morecambe, Lancs, Sandylands, United Methodist Chapel. 2 manuals
1911	Reeth, North Yorks, Wesleyan Chapel. 2 manuals
1911	Barnoldswick, Lancs, Primitive Methodist Chapel. 2 manuals
1912	Bradford, West Yorks, Wilsden, Primitive Methodist. 2 manuals
1912	Lothersdale, Lancs, Parish Church. 2 manuals
1913	Middlesbrough, Woodlands Road, Wesleyan Chapel. 1 manual
1913	Blackburn, Lancs, Read. St. John's Parish Church. 2 manuals
1914	Skipton, West Yorks. Congregational Chapel. 3 manuals
1919	Halifax, Yorks, Southowram. Primitive Methodist Chapel. 2 manuals

St. Michael's Parish Church
Foulridge, Lancs

This church is built on a slight elevation by the side of Lake Burwain, where in the Spring and Summer months sheep and lambs wander at will through the churchyard. The main architectural feature is the sturdy bell tower coupled with a collection of smaller turrets and a variety of roof levels. The church was built in 1904 the Church Building Society donating £100 towards its cost. Internally the roof is timber lined and supported by bracketed tie-beam trusses. The nave consists of five arched bays supported on stone octagonal columns with moulded caps. The interior is finished in rough-cut stone presenting a sturdy appearance. The wood-work is of English oak in a simple design and the windows are of plain glass.

The organ is positioned in the north chancel bay. Built in 1907 at a cost of £400 by Messrs. Laycock & Bannister, Aire Street, Crosshills. Yorks. The facade pipework dominates the chancel area, the casework above the impost level having a large overhang from the top of the console. The Open Diapason is in prospect and is of a very large scale made from zinc with polished metal 'bay leaf' mouths. This chancel organ chamber appears to have presented some tonal difficulties, and in order to overcome this the display pipework has been conveyanced-off the main windchest in order to project the sound into the body of the building. The result has, unfortunately, created an inartistic appearance. The side elevation faces into the north aisle and is a smaller version of the chancel arrangement.

Fig. 34. St. Michael's Parish Church, Foulridge, Lancs. Organ built by Messrs. Laycock & Bannister, Crosshills.

Photo. B. Hughes

St. Michael's Parish Church, Foulridge, Lancs

Organ by Laycock & Bannister of Crosshills. 1907. Cost £400.

Great CC-A		**Swell**		**Pedal** CCC-F	
Open Diapason	8'	Bourdon	16'	Bourdon	16'
Gamba	8'	Open Diapason	8'	Open Diapason	16'
Dulciana	8'	Viol d'Orchestra	8'		
Hohl Flute	8'	Rohr Flute	8'	**Couplers**	
Principal	4'	Voix Celeste (T.C.)		Swell to Great	
Harmonic Flute	4'	Gemshorn	4'	Great to Pedal	
		Fifteenth	2'	Swell to Pedal	
		Cornopean	8'	Swell Super	
		Oboe	8'	Octave	8'
		Tremulant			

3 Combination pedals to Great & Pedal: 3 combination pedals to Swell

St. John's Parish Church
Read, Burnley, Lancs

Built in a pleasant setting in the centre of the village, St. John's Church is designed in the Early English style, the chancel terminating in an apse. The roof is supported by a scissors truss, the internal woodwork being of selected pitch pine. At the west end is some attractive arcading which forms the baptistry.

    The organ built by Messrs. Laycock & Bannister, is positioned in the north bay of the chancel behind the choir. It was erected in 1912 and cost £275. The action is mechanical, the only modification being replacement of the Piccolo by a Fifteenth on the Great.

St. John's, Read, Burnley. Built 1912 by Laycock & Bannister.

Great CC-A		**Pedal** CCC-F		Swell	**Pedal**	
Open Diapason	8'	Violin Diapason	8'		Bourdon	16'
Dulciana	8'	Salicional	8'		Bass Flute	8'
Hohl Flute	8'	Rohr Flute	8'			
Principal	4'	Gemshorn	4'			
Fifteenth	2'	Mixture	2rks			
		Oboe	8'			
		Tremulant				

Couplers
Great to Pedal
Swell to Pedal
Swell to Great
Swell Super Octave
2 combination pedals to Great and Pedal
2 combination pedals to Swell

Fig. 35. St. John's Parish Church, Read. Burnley, Lancashire. Organ by Laycock & Bannister. Crosshills. 1912.

After the end of hostilities (1914-18) the Aire Street workshop continued to flourish, there was however, a dearth of tradesmen; many did not return to the craft in the post-war years. In the 'shop books' for this period are several interesting entries. They throw some light on the management of the business at Aire Street, Crosshills. For example, in the early 1900s, there was a Christmas Box payment of two-shillings and sixpence. The water rate for the building was one-shilling per month. Board and lodging for the men erecting the organ in St. Catherine's Church, Burnley was calculated at £5-8s-0d per week. In 1903, it is noted that the Christmas Box payment was now fifteen shillings. On April 6th, 1904. Henry (Harry) Bannister Jr, commenced his apprenticeship; and on February 11th in the same year another apprentice Cecil Horner was taken into the firm.

The Aire Street workshop was illuminated by gas lighting throughout and an item for gas mantles is entered in the 'shop books' at one-shilling and one-penny for 5 mantles. Additional machinery was acquired at this time which included a lathe, boring and screwing machines and a casting bench. No evidence has been found that Laycock & Bannisters supplied metal pipework to the trade; it is presumed that any casting was done specifically for their own use, or this side of the business was not a success.

The finances of the business was now in the care of the Craven Bank in Skipton (later Martin's Bank) and a balance sheet for January 16th, 1905 provides the firm's assets.[9]

June 16th, 1905. Balance sheet Messrs. Laycock & Bannister.

Liabilities

Amount owing to Keighley Building Society	£181-0s-0d.
Amount owing to sundry tradesman	£71-17s-0d
To balance	£2,592-16s-3d
	£2,845-13s-3d

Assets

Value of shop & yard	£725-0s-0d
Timber & other stock	£1,242-0s-7d
Amount of book debts	£351-10s-0d
Balance to Craven Bank	£527-6s-2d
Petty Cash	6s-6d
	£2, 845-13s-3d

Fig. 36. The Glusburn Institute Baptist Chapel Glusburn, West Yorks.

GLUSBURN INSTITUTE, showing the addition of a mission hall for the Baptist church.

The Glusburn Institute Baptist Chapel, Glusburn, West Yorkshire

Perhaps the finest building in the Glusburn area and known as the 'Institute' was opened in October 1892. Built by Sir Jeremiah C Horsfall of Fairfield Hall; owner of Hayfield Mill and a local benefactor. The 'old mill' was powered by an undershot water wheel and in 1827 a second wheel was added, when the mill was extended and operated by an additional inlet (this wheel survived until 1938). By 1835 Horsfall had installed a steam turbine. The mill suffered through the disturbances of some 'luddite' action during its modernisation and some spinning mules which Sir Jeremiah had ordered from Manchester, passing through Colne on horse drawn conveyances, were intercepted by a mob and destroyed, the carriers being forced to return to Manchester.

Sir Jeremiah Horsfall built the Glusburn Institute as an educational, social and religious centre for the life of the village. Some years later a Baptist Chapel was added, built in a style to match the existing architecture. The heating for both Institute and Chapel was provided from the mill which was situated directly opposite. Heating pipes were branched off from the mill boilers and carried under the roadway and into the Institute buildings providing continuous heating at a very economical cost.

In 1914 Messrs. Laycock & Bannister were commissioned to build an organ for the Institute Baptist Chapel. The church is built on a rectangular plan with seating for approximately two hundred people. The interior furnishings have a simple arrangement of central table, pulpit and lectern all positioned on a raised platform. All the woodwork including the organ casework is of English oak and natural lighting is provided by windows of plain glass with coloured margins. The organ is positioned behind the pulpit and occupies the whole of the end wall of the building. The casework is panelled to impost level, the display pipework is supported on a curved framework and arranged in four 'flats'. The drawstop console is placed on the north wall, the action throughout is on the firms pressure pneumatic patent. The console which has no playing aids is nevertheless not without two interesting features. The tremulant on the Swell is brought on and off by the pistons placed over the top manual. The roll top cover is fitted with 'tear drop' handles which were also used as 'dress' handles in the undertaking side of the organ building business.

The Baptist Chapel, Glusburn Institute. Built 1914

Manuals CC-C: Pedal CCC-F

Great		**Swell**		**Pedal**	
Open Diapason	8'	Violin Diapason	8'	Bourdon	16'
Dulciana	8'	Salicional	8'	Bass Flute	8'
Lieblich Gedact	8'	Rhor Flute	8'		
Principal	4'	Voix Celeste (TC)	8'	**Couplers**	
		Oboe	8'	Swell Super Octave	
Tremulant				Swell to Great	
				Swell to Pedal	
				Great to Pedal	

Fig. 37. The Glusburn Institute Baptist Chapel. Organ by Laycock & Bannister. 1914.

Fig. 38. The Glusburn Institute Baptist Chapel, West Yorks. Organ by Laycock & Bannister built 1914. The console.

Fig. 39. English Oak console cover fitted with 'tear drop' handles used also for coffin fittings made by the organ building firm.

Shortly after the completion of the Glusburn Institute organ, William Laycock retired from business and was succeeded by his son William Herbert Laycock with Charles Bannister remaining as the second partner in the business.

Between 1914 – 1919 fifteen new instruments were completed, these were difficult years with the economy recovering from the effects of war. The commissions completed over this period included.[10]

1914	Hawes, North Yorks, Wesleyan Chapel. 2 manuals
1915	Keighley, West Yorks, Crossroads, St. James' Parish Church. 2 manuals. Cost £500. Hydraulic engine £45
1917	Wortley, West Yorks, The Parish Church. 2 manuals. Cost £479-15s-0d
1918	Cononley, West Yorks. Baptist Chapel. 2 manuals Cost £260
1919	Pendleton, Pendle, Lancs, Primitive Methodist. 3 manuals. Cost £400
1920	Halifax, Yorks. Trinity Wesleyan Chapel. 3 manuals
1921	Leeds, Yorks. Little Holbeck. St. John's Parish Church. 3 manuals
1923	Otley, West Yorks. Wesleyan Chapel. 3 manuals
1924	Crosshills, West Yorks. United Methodist Chapel. 3 manuals
1925	Kilburn, East Yorks. The Parish Church. 2 manuals
1928	Nelson, Lancs. St. John's Parish Church. 3 manuals

1919 was a significant year in the life of the Laycock & Bannister firm, instruments were built for the Primitive Methodist Chapel, Pendleton, Pendle; Ben Rhydding, Wesleyan Chapel, West Yorks; and St. Stephen's Parish Church, Burnley. Also a theatre organ was in the planning stages for The Picture House, Crosshills. The firm had tuned the piano and harmonium used to accompany the silent films for a fee of £2 for many years. Unfortunately, this project never came to fruition.

William Laycock, who had been in retirement for several years, died after a short illness. The funeral arrangements were in the care of Laycock & Bannister and are entered in the 'Shop Books' for 1919. May 31st.[11]

Hearse and five cabs	£3-12s-0d	(£3.60p)
Opening grave and walling, attending at funeral	£1-17s-6d	(£1.87$\frac{1}{2}$p)
Bricks flags and mortar	18s-6d	(92$\frac{1}{2}$p)
Surplus earth	3s-6d	(17$\frac{1}{2}$p)
Refixing curb stones	3s-6d	(17$\frac{1}{2}$p)
Trustees. Minister. Caretaker	5s-0d	(25p)
80 memorandum cards	£1-10s-0d	(£1.50p)
6 widows notices	2s-6d	(12$\frac{1}{2}$p)
Oak coffin fumed and polished, lined and wadded, best shroud, solid brass furniture and brass plate	£15-0s-0d	
	£17-1s-0d	**(£17.05p)**

The Craven Herald in May 1919 reported on the death of William Laycock and an abridged version of the newspaper article is given:[12]

"The death took place on Wednesday week at the age of 74 years of William Laycock of Ravensville, Aire Street, Crosshills. He was an active senior partner in the organ building firm of Messrs. Laycock & Bannister, owned formerly by his father John Laycock. William Laycock was a typical Yorkshireman and the many organs built by his firm will doubtless keep his memory alive for many years. Mr. Laycock took little part in public affairs, though he was closely connected with the Crosshills Wesleyan Church and Sunday School and was a Trustee for many years. As the cortege entered the church the organist Mr. Walter Thornton played "O Rest In The Lord" (Elijah) and at the close the 'Dead March' in Saul. The services at the house and church were conducted by the Revd. H.P. Thomas of Silsden: Messrs. Laycock & Bannister were in charge of the arrangements."

Laycock & Bannister's middle period between 1925-39 was a very busy time. Mechanical blowing was in fast decline, hydraulic engines had been in use for many years, and where there was adequate water pressure, this form of blowing provided a reliable and steady wind pressure.

Laycock & Bannisters supplied hydraulic engines at a cost of £45. These were followed by

Fig. 40. Members of the Laycock organ building family of Crosshills. West Yorkshire.
Back row: Maggi Laycock, John Herbert Laycock.
Front row: Anne Laycock, William Laycock, Ann Laycock (neé Riddiough), Clara Laycock.

electrical fan blowers; and from the Aire Street workshop emerged the firm's own development, the 'Layban' organblower.

The 'Layban' blowing fans operated from direct coupled motors with a specially extended shaft of large diameter with ring oiled bearings. The impellor was constructed of cross battened wooden blades of relatively crude construction. These were housed in a roughly constructed casing. The motors were required to cope with a very high starting torque on a low speed. DC machines were shunt wound 110 volts – 850 volts and AC machines two or three phase 100-550 volts. Automatic push button starters were fitted to the organ consoles. The electrical motors were supplied by Horace Green, Engineers of Cononly, West Yorks. These blowing units are recorded as being silent in operation and having a reliable life, but maintenance was a difficult process. The 'Layban' blower was designed and patented by Mr John Williams Bannister.

Fig. 41. Sections of the 'Layban' organblower. and patented by – Mr. John Williams Bannister.

Over many years the firm of Laycock & Bannister received many letters and testimonials from clergy, private clients and professional musicians. All who wrote in favourable terms, expressed their satisfaction with the quality of the firm's workmanship.[13]

Woodbridge, Ripon
I recently had the pleasure of playing on the new three manual organ erected by Messrs. Laycock & Bannister at the U.M. Church, Cross Hills, Keighley.

The instrument impressed me by the excellence of its tone and the perfection of its mechanism. The orchestral stops showed voicing of a very delicate order and the Diapason tone was admirable.

If this organ may be regarded as characteristic of the firm's work in general, I can with confidence recommend Laycock & Bannister as worthy of wide support.
Charles Henry-Moody, CBE, Mus.Doc. FRCO, Organist of Ripon Cathedral, 1 Headingly Mount Kirkstall Lane, Leeds.

Fig. 42. Layban blower plate from blowing plant manufactured by Messrs. Laycock & Bannister. West Yorks. Plate.

I have much pleasure in stating that I gave an organ recital at the Roscoe Place Wesleyan Chapel, Leeds, upon the organ built by Messrs. Laycock & Bannister, and found it most satisfactory. The tone is good; the stops are well voiced, individually and collectively; the action is quite up to date and reliable.
Edward Cuthbert Bairstow, Mus.D., F.R.C.O. Organist and Choirmaster, Leeds Parish Church. Talma, Victoria Park.

I opened an organ at Keighley recently, and gave a performance at Burnley, upon instruments from the factory of Messrs. Laycock & Bannister. I was well pleased with both organs, and thought them artistic and admirable in every way. In fact, far above the average good instruments I play upon.

The tone is bright, pure, sonorous, and the mechanism exact and responsive. In both cases the instruments were moderate in price.
James Kendrick Pyne, Mus.Doc., F.R.C.O. Organist (Cathedral, Town Hall, and University) Manchester.

Dear Sirs,
I have much pleasure in affording my sincere testimony to the excellence of the organ built for Bolton Abbey. They have more than fulfilled my expectations of their work in carrying out every particular of my specification, both as to tone and workmanship. More conscientious builders I have never been connected with, and can confidently recommend them to build an instrument of the kind that may be required, especially for use in Divine Worship.
William Spark, Mus.Doc., Organist. Leeds Town Hall.

By this time Charles Bannister was looking towards retirement. His two sons (always known as Harry and Johnny) were now sufficiently mature to take a serious interest in the future of the firm. John Herbert Laycock (grandson of the founder) was still in the business, He appears to have preferred to stay at his workbench and to leave the administrative side to others. However, within a few years the Bannister side of the partnership begins to come into prominence.

In 1929, significant changes are taking place within the establishment, brought about by the death of the second partner and founder member.

The Craven Herald. Friday, December 13th. 1929. [14]
"Mr Charles Bannister of Calstock House and of the firm of Laycock & Bannister organbuilders died on Tuesday night at the age of 75. Up to a few years ago he was an active partner in the firm. Himself and Mr. John Laycock had founded the business at West Closes, Glusburn in 1840, the business being removed to its present premises in 1892.

"Mr. Bannister had served his apprenticeship with the founder, and later was taken into partnership. Many examples of the firm's organ building are to be found in places of worship in the neighbourhood and further afield. Mr Bannister leaves a widow, two sons and a daughter."

Between 1929 – 1938. Evelyn Mary Moore (neé Walmsley) became company secretary, she has many happy memories and stories of her years with the Laycock & Bannister firm. Evelyn came from a musical background; her father was drummer in the Kildwick Band together with a brother and uncle who played instruments in the same brass band. Her sister, Bertha, became a trained singer. Later when the family obtained a piano, the occasion was looked upon as a great event; particularly as it was a German instrument and purchased from Green's Music Suppliers in Silsden. The problem then arose as to the transportation of the instrument, which was finally solved by the use of a canal barge; also the Leeds & Liverpool Canal flowed close by the end of May Street, Evelyn's home in the village of Farnhill, Yorks. Evelyn recalls, the piano was delivered with much ceremony, all the street turned out to witness its arrival with willing hands to push the heavy iron framed instrument into its home. Now in retirement at her home in Keighley, Evelyn recalls the names of several members of the Laycock & Bannister staff in the mid 1930s; William Herbert Laycock, Harry and Johnny Bannister others were Cedric Laycock (William Herbert's son), Ernest Longbottom, Benjamin Blackstone, Claud Whiteoak, Thomas Armstrong, Eric Hargreaves, Charles Waite; Arthur-Sellers, Kenneth Seward and William Pierce, who

Fig. 43. Evelyn Mary Moore (nee Walmesley) living in Keighley, Yorkshire. Company secretary for Laycock & Bannister, Organbuilders 1929-38.

remember that the late 1920s was not an easy time in the organ building trade. The wages for a tuner were fourteen shillings per week (70p). William also remembers the days when he tuned the organ at Laneshaw Bridge Methodist Chapel.Colne. Lancashire, when he would breakfast at 5am in order to take the 6-30a.m train from Kildwick to Nelson. Extra allowances for travelling were meagre, with either 6d sixpence ($2^1/2$p) or 1/– one-shilling (5p) for tea. Payments for overtime were at the normal rate for the first two hours i.e. two-shillings and nine pence per hour ($14^1/2$p) and beyond this the workman was paid at time and a quarter; with 1/6d: one-shilling and sixpence ($7^1/2$p) for dinner and 6d sixpence (5p) for tea.

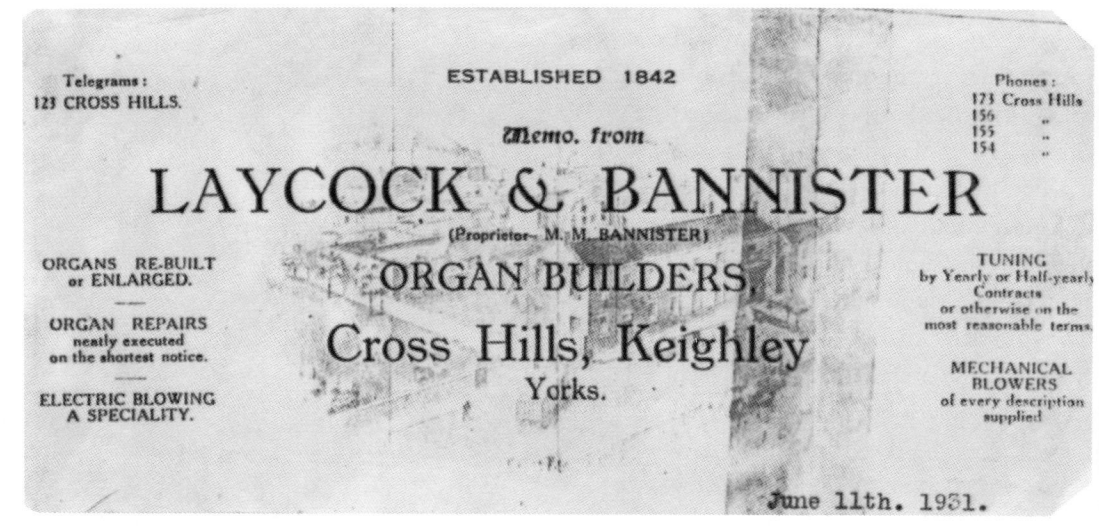

Fig.44. Messrs. Laycock & Bannister letterheads 1931. M.M.Bannister is now shown as Proprietor.

By the early 1930s the control of the business appears to be in the hands of the Bannister partnership. The letter heading of the firm is now styled LAYCOCK & BANNISTER. ORGANBUILDERS. CROSSHILLS, KEIGHLEY, YORKS. Proprietor M.M. Bannister, (Martha Maria Bannister wife of the late Charles Bannister). Harry Bannister now prepared the specifications of the instruments and also the costings along with a large amount of on-site work in the churches. Johnny Bannister had a small room situated at the end of the gallery over the loading bay. Here equipped with the voicing machine he was responsible for the tonal success of Laycock & Bannister organs. When the workshop was particularly busy both of the Bannister brothers would arrive on-site to work on the erection of an instrument. Evelyn Moore also recalls that William Herbert Laycock seemed to have been content to remain at his bench, very much in the way his grandfather had done and rarely came into the office on administrative matters.

The metal pipework was supplied by Messrs. Rogers of Bramley, Leeds and the reeds for the orchestral sound of the instruments were obtained from Messrs. Palmer's of London; the names of two timber suppliers have also been entered into the 'shop books' Messrs. Riddiough of Colne Lancs (into whose family Mr. William Laycock had married) supplied softwoods, pine and deal. Messrs. Watson of Bradford, Yorks; provided mahogany and selected pitch pine.[15]

Along with the tasks of general workshop practice several members of the staff were allocated specific work.

John Proctor, now in retirement at Cononly, West Yorks worked for Laycock & Bannister for more than twenty years making wooden pipes and erecting instruments on-site: Benjamin Blackstone specialised in making soundboards and swell boxes also doing much on-site work and William Pierce who had worked for the firm from 1927 until his retirement, made coupling blocks for pneumatic actions. He also travelled over a wide area covering a very large tuning round built up by the firm over many years which included Scotland and the Isle of Man.

St. German's Parish Church, Peel, Isle of Man (now the cathedral) was completed in August 1884, to a design by the architect Thomas Barry of Liverpool. Built of local stone, the internal supporting columns are of octagonal and circular sections and of a harder Cheshire stone. There are some interesting stained glass windows; one depicting the Last Supper commemorates Mark Hilesley, who translated The Bible into Manx. The choir was provided with new stalls in 1935 all with 'poppy head' carvings.

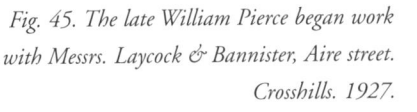

Fig. 45. The late William Pierce began work with Messrs. Laycock & Bannister, Aire street. Crosshills. 1927.

Fig. 46. John Proctor (retired) pipe maker with Laycock & Bannister.

Fig. 47. The last of the Laycock line of Crosshills organbuilders. Mr. Cedric William Laycock with his wife Dorothy now retired in Silsden, Yorkshire.

Messrs. Laycock & Bannister provided a new organ situated on the south side of the choir, to the following specification.

Manuals. CC-A 58 notes

Great		**Swell**		**Pedal**	
Open Diapason	8'	Open Diapason	8'	Open Diapason	16'
Clarabella	8'	Stopped Diapason	8'	Bourdon	16'
Gamba	8'	Salicional	8'	Principal	8'
Principal	4'	Voix Celeste	8'	Bass Flute	8'
Harmonic Flute	4'	Gemshorn	4'	Choral Bass	
Twelfth	2 2/3	Piccolo	2'		
Fifteenth	2'	Mixture	3rks		
Mixture	3rks	Contra Fagotta	16'		
Trumpet	8'	Cornopean	8'		
		Clarion	4'		

Couplers

Swell to Great	Swell Sub Octave	Great to Pedal
Great to Pedal	Swell Octave	Swell to Pedal
Melodic Bass	Tremulant	

This was a typical church organ that one would expect to find from a provincial English organbuilder of the immediate post-war years. There was a normal Diapason to Mixture chorus and a single chorus reed, a trumpet on the great division. On the swell organ (the enclosed section) we find a partial string and flute chorus and a moderately powerful 3 rank mixture and a chorus of reeds at 16'-8'-4' pitches. The pedal organ is typical of its period, but with the inclusion of a metal Principal 8' and a Choral Bass 4' we find some positive effort to develop the pedal organ on more modern lines. The inclusion of a Melodic Bass is unusual in an instrument of this size. It is more commonly to be found in small chamber instruments. This stop provides the lowest note in a given chord for the left hand. It is most useful for a pianist who may not be conversant with the pedal organ.

Other work carried out by the firm in the Isle of Man included the Methodist Church, Kirk Michael; Ballath Parish Church (one manual with a divided soundboard); St. Olaves Parish Church, Ramsey; Loch Promenade Congregational Church, Douglas; Station Road Methodist Church, Port Erin: St. Matthew's Parish Church, Douglas; The Parish Church, Bride; and King William's College Chapel, Peel.

During the 'middle period' in the firms' history (1925-38) electricity had been introduced into their consoles, either in a direct form between key and pallet or as electrical relays to operate the electro-pneumatic action. The firm now produced detached consoles whereby the keyboard could be separated from the pipework, thus allowing the organist to hear to better effect the tonal colours of the registration he may have selected and also it was advantageous in controlling a choir and congregation. The pneumatic actions made by Messrs. Laycock & Bannister whether operated completely by wind pressure or electro-pneumatic were all of the pressure type.

A selection of the firms' work at this period included instruments for:
Wilsden Methodist Church, Bradford, Yorkshire
St. Stephen's Parish Church, Blackburn, Lancashire
Morten Parish Church, Bingley, Yorkshire
United Methodist Church, Crosshills, Yorkshire
Trinity Wesleyan Church, Halifax, Yorkshire
The Wesleyan Church, Hawes, Yorkshire
Lindley Wesleyan Church, Huddersfield, Yorkshire
Private Residence, Mr. H Smith, Bingley, Yorkshire
Lees Wesleyan Church, Keighley, Yorkshire
St. John's Parish Church, Keighley, Yorkshire
Heysham Home of Rest, Morecambe, Lancashire
St. John's Parish Church, Nelson, Lancashire
Primitive Methodist Church, Skipton, Yorkshire
Private Residence of Mr John Altham 'Greycourt' Reedley, Burnley, Lancashire
Roscoe Place Wesleyan Church, Leeds, Yorkshire

Greycourt Reedley, Burnley, Lancashire is a large detached house set in spacious grounds and well kept garden. The instrument was sold during the post war years shortly after the owner's death when all trace of it was lost and of the music room there is only an outline of the foundations. Kenneth Seward, for may years on the staff of Laycock & Bannister describes the music room as: built onto the side elevation of the house and containing along with the organ a grand piano and billiard table. He also mentioned with affection the kindness and hospitality he received from Mr. John Altham during several visits in order to tune the instrument at 'Greycourt'.

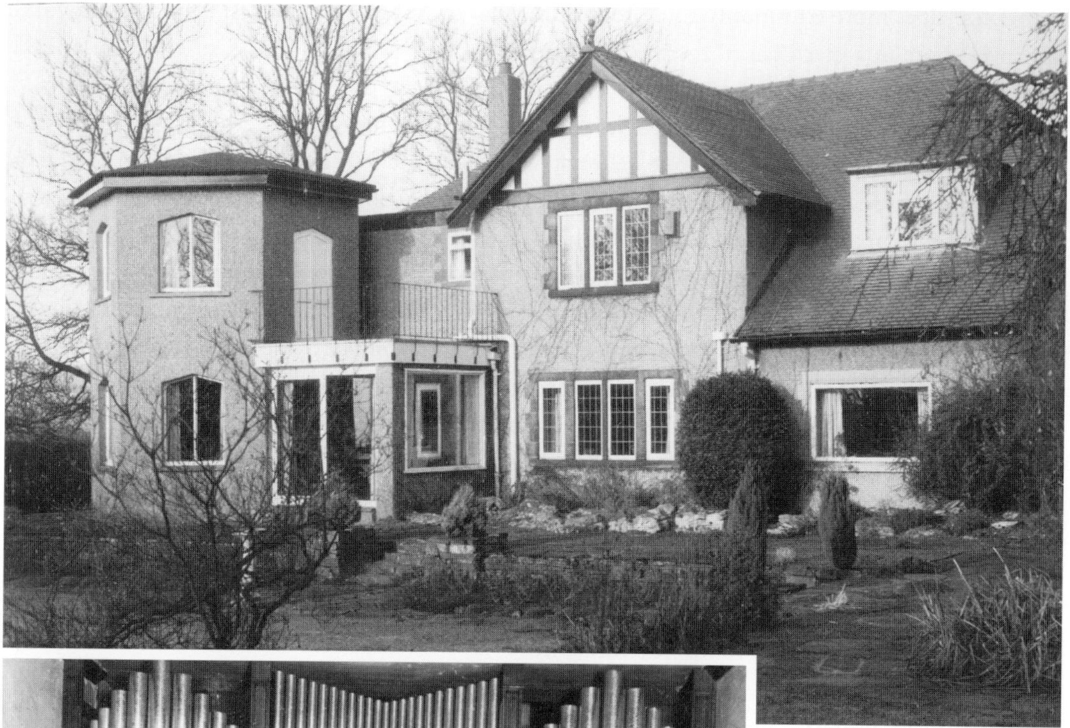

Photo B. Hughes. By kind permission of Mr & Mrs Ratcliffe

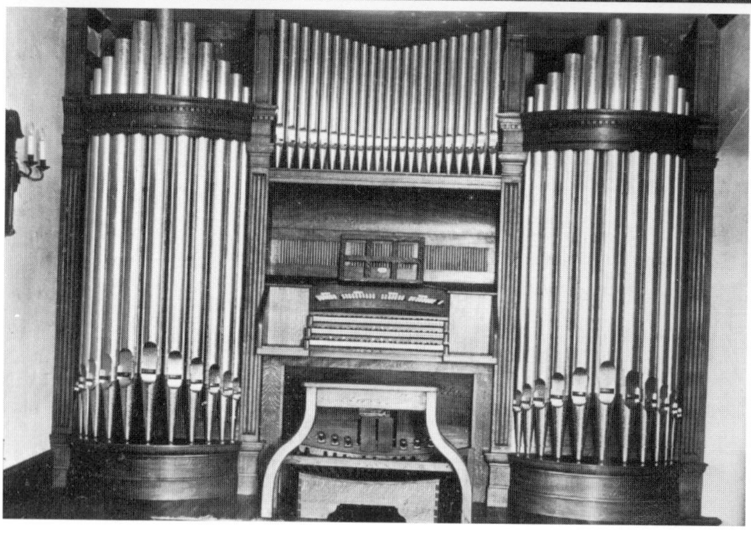

Photo W.Neville Blakey. Archive, Brierfield, Nelson, Lancs

Fig. 48. 'Greycourt' Reedley, Burnley, Lancashire.

Fig. 49. 'Greycourt' Reedley, Burnley, Lancashire. The music room with Laycock & Bannister organ with all electrical action.

"Greycourt:", Reedley, Burnley. Lancs. Built by Messrs. Laycock & Bannister with an all electrical stopkey console. Manuals. CC-C. 61 notes.

Great		**Swell**	
Double Open Diapason	16'	Violin Diapason	8'
Open Diapason	8'	Viol d' Orchestra	8'
Dulciana	8'	Voix Celeste	8'
Clarabella	8'	Lieblich Gedact	8'
Flute Traverso	4'	Lieblich Flute	4'
		Horn	8'
Pedal. CCC-F. 30 notes.		Orchestral Oboe	8'
Contra Viola	16'	Tremulant	
Bourdon	16'	**Choir.**	
Flute Bass	8'	Viola	8'
		Rhor Flute	8'
		Wald Flute	4'
		Clarinet	8'
		Tremulant	

Couplers Swell to Choir: Swell Octave: Swell to Great: Swell Sub Octave: Choir Sub Octave Choir Octave: Choir to Great: Swell to Pedal
Great to Pedal: Choir to Pedal.
Accessories 5 pistons to Great: 3 pistons to Swell: 3 toe pistons to Great:
3 toe pistons to Swell:
R.C. Pedalboard.
'Layban' blower.

At this period the firm received a commission which resulted in the building of their largest instrument up to that time. This was for Roscoe Place Wesleyan Church, Leeds. The award of this commission caused great excitement at the workshop and Henry (Harry) Bannister insisted that John Bannister should make models of all the various actions before the project was started. John (always known as 'Johnny') was particularly inventive and the models were put out for demonstration for their neat and clever execution.

Roscoe Place Wesleyan Church, Leeds
Built by Messrs. Laycock & Bannister. Crosshills, Yorkshire.

3 manuals and pedals 45 drawstops. Manuals CC-C. 61 notes. Pedals CCC-F. 30 notes

Great		**Swell**	
Bourdon	16' wood & metal	Bourdon	16' wood
Large Open Diapason	8' metal	Open Diapason	8' metal
Gamba	8' metal	Stopped Diapason	8' wood and metal
Hohl Flute	8' wood & metal	Viol d' Orchestra	8' metal
Harmonic Flute	4' metal	Voix Celeste	8' metal
Principal	4' metal	Principal	4' metal
Fifteenth	2' metal	Mixture	3rks metal
Mixture	3rks metal	Horn	8' metal
Trumpet	8' metal	Oboe	8' metal
		Tremulant	

Fig. 50. Roscoe Place Wesleyan Church, Leeds

Photo. Laycock & Bannister Catalogue.

Choir

Violin Diapason	8'	metal
Stopped Diapason	8'	metal
Salicional	8'	metal
Lieblich Flute	4'	metal
Spitz Flute	4'	metal
Piccolo Flute	2'	metal
Clarionet	8'	metal

Pedal

Open Diapason 32' wood (quinted)	
Open Diapason	16' wood
Bourdon	16' wood
Violone	16' wood
Violoncello	8' metal
Flute Bass	8' wood
Octave coupler acting on all pedal stops	

Couplers

Swell to Great: Swell to Great Super Octave: Swell to Great Sub Octave: Great Sub Octave: Great Super Octave: Swell Sub Octave: Swell Super Octave: Swell to Choir: Choir to Great: Choir to Pedals: Swell to Pedals: Great to Pedals

Pistons

(double acting) Tremulant- On/Off: Swell to Great: Swell to Pedals: Great to Pedals: Pedal Bourdon: Small swell chorus: Large swell chorus: Full Organ: Combination pedals to Great & Pedal. Pneumatic action throughout. Casework of polished pitch pine. Drawstops at 45º degrees. Pipes 2,097.

By the closing years of the firms' 'middle period' the political clouds were darkening over Europe and outbreak of war seemed inevitable. By the end of 1939 the firm had lost one of its senior partners and grandson of its founder. *The Craven Herald & Pioneer* December 1st. 1939.[16] "Mr. John Herbert Laycock of 'Ravensville', Crosshills of the firm of Laycock & Bannister organbuilders had a lifetimes association with musical interests in the district, his family having traced their history into the 17th century. His grandfather John Laycock had founded the firm which is now continued by members of two families, their work is to be found over a wide area of England, Isle of Man, Wales and Scotland. John Herbert Laycock held the position of organist at St. John's Methodist Church, Crosshills for over 35 years, and his influence will long be felt. He had a fine artistic taste and was keenly devoted to literature. Mr. Laycock who was sixty years of age had been married twice, his second wife dying some three years ago. He leaves a son and daughter, the former who is now serving in the forces. Service in St. John's Church was conducted by the Revd. S Paul Hadley. The hymns chosen were 'God of my life through all my days' to the Tune 'Saul' and 'In heavenly love abiding' tune Penlan. These being the favourite hymns of Mr Laycock. Miss. E Thornton was the organist".

During the war years and throughout the difficulties and problems of food rationing, tea and sugar for the men, supply of wood, screws and fittings, the firm kept active. Both Harry and Johnny were inventive and were no doubt planning its future for the post-War era.

They had produced a novel idea for which a patent had been applied for a pedalboard

80 John Laycock

designed to the Royal College of Organists regulations. This pedalboard was designed to be attached to any pianoforte, and enabled the player to practice the pedal part in three stave compositions. This was ideal for music students who had not a ready access to an organ console.

Frank Bannister produced various kinds of novelties one of which took the form of a jewellery box, in which there were two small eyelets in the lid. There being no other apparent means of opening it, Frank or Johnny would offer 10/– ten-shillings to anyone who could succeed in opening or successfully locking it. The box consisted of three separate compartments. The central section was fitted with a small pneumatic bellows (cuckoo clock type). When the box was closed, blowing into one of the slots in the lid caused the bellows to inflate and so released the lid. To reverse the movement, one sucked at the adjacent slot and exhausted the bellows which engaged a small catch thus locking the lid.

Frank Bannister also tells of his experience when he and an apprentice were tuning the organ in the Chapel of Wakefield jail. He was asked if they carried any files in their tool box, and these were counted before entering and on leaving. The apprentice's age caused a regulation problem, as he was too young to be on prison premises. This was solved by sending for one of the prisoners, who played the organ on Sundays. He acted as key holder whilst Frank tuned inside the organ. At the end of the day Frank Bannister left the prisoner ten cigarettes.

The workshop now passed into the control of Charles Bannister's two sons, Henry and John. War in Europe had commenced and amongst those of the staff who had enlisted into the forces were included Henry Bannister's son Frank (later to become managing director) who was now serving in the Royal Navy as a stoker; and Cedric W. Laycock great-grandson of the founder. There was now scarcely any real organ building taking place, but the firm had built up a large tuning area, and the remaining staff were kept employed by tuning and maintenance and small repairs to existing instruments.

With the continuation of hostilities, shortage of materials and reduction in staff Harry Bannister now decided to move into smaller premises and the fine purpose built workshop in Aire Street, Crosshills was sold. (It is now converted into five attractive terraced houses).

A smaller workshop was now opened only a short distance away and situated along the same street; here work continued until the cessation of hostilities and the return of some members of the organ building staff.

Following in the traditions of the founder, Harry Bannister was also a woodturner, receiving his tuition from an experienced local craftsman Israel Dawson (this workshop founded in 1862 still produces fine turnery as W & J.R. Thompson (Woodturners) Ltd. Crosshills, Keighley, Yorks). In later years Harry sustained an injury whilst working at the lathe, which cost him the loss of an eye and a glass one with excellent matching colouring had to be fitted. As a member of the Silsden Conservative Club it was Harry's regular habit to call for a drink and a chat at the end of a day in the workshop. On one occasion a colleague invited him to a game of billiards, for a

Opposite: Fig. 51. Piano with Pedal Attachment. Produced and fitted by Messrs. Laycock & Bannister, Crosshills, Yorks.

small wager of ten shillings but mentioning that he felt handicapped as he only had one eye. Whereupon, to his opponent's surprise Harry Bannister, removing his own glass eye and placing it on the edge of the billiard table, countered with the remark, "Right, now we can both start equal".

Harry Bannister received a complaint from a chapel that 'the organ sounded out of tune' almost immediately after the tuner had paid a visit. This was in the days when there were still a number of instruments blown by hand. Several visits were made in order to correct the fault; but the complaints continued. Finally, during one visit, Mr. Bannister re-arranged the bellows weights on top of the reservoir in a particular order and made a note of their placement. After a further complaint of defective tuning it was discovered that the weights were not in the same position as left by Mr. Bannister; who then enquired who was the organblower and was told. "Oh, a young lad in the village. He's reliable every Sunday; but a bit simple'. Mr. Bannister replied. "Not so simple. He knows how to make his work easier by removing some of the bellows weights and putting 'em back after service".

With the cessation of hostilities in 1945 there was a gradual return of members of the staff and also an increase in work. Many instruments had suffered from a lack of maintenance and the main source of work for the next few years was much needed repairs and occasional rebuilding as money was not in plentiful supply.

However, the following five year period saw a decided upturn in work and the return from the forces of some regular members of the staff which included Frank Bannister; Cedric William Laycock and Kenneth Seward. This period was however tinged with internal problems due to various disagreements between the two partners, mostly regarding finance. William Pierce (bench-hand and tuner) recalls witnessing several quarrels that arose to such a degree and resulting in bellows weights and other materials being hurled across the workshop, and on occasions at each other. A break in the partnership was inevitable. Johnny Bannister left the firm taking with him one or two members of the staff. The partnership was dissolved with an agreement that the outgoing partner should not set-up in business within a five mile radius of Crosshills. Unfortunately, this agreement was not honoured and Johnny Bannister opened a small workshop in the vacated building of the Crosshills Liberal Club, only a short distance away in the centre of the township. Here he traded under the name of Bannister Organs until his death in 1960.

Craven Herald & Pioneer. Friday, May 16th. 1960.[17]
"Crosshills has lost a life long and well known resident by the death at the age of 77 of John Williams Bannister of "Clovelley", Park Road, Crosshills. His father, the late Mr. Charles Bannister, was one of the founders of the organ building firm of Laycock and Bannister, a business which was started in West Closes, Glusburn. Mr John Bannister started in the business when he left school and continued until his father's death, when he, along with his brother Henry, were made partners. Later Mr John W. Bannister dissolved the partnership, forming an organ building company of his own in the old Liberal Club buildings on Milligan Fields,

Crosshills, where he continued in business until his final illness. Mr. Bannister was for many years a member of Crosshills Tennis Club and a regular player until he reached the age of 70. He had won several cups and other trophies, proof of his prowess at the game. He had a life long association with the Ebenezer Church, Crosshills. Mr. Bannister leaves a widow, a married daughter and a grandson. The funeral service was conducted by the Revd. A Taylor Clarke at Crosshills Methodist Church; the organist was Mrs G Henderson. Committal was at Skipton Crematorium".

Mr. Harry Bannister was now in full control with the assistance of his son Frank, who was taking an active part in running the business. They had also reinstated those few members of the staff who had left the firm during its internal troubles.

A commission was now received to transfer an instrument built by the firm some years previously for the residence of Mr. Henry Smith of 'Butterfield' House, Bingley, Yorkshire, who was in business as a manufacturer of woodworking machinery. When first commissioned this was the firm's first all electric stopkey console coupled with an electro-pneumatic action to the soundboards, the pneumatic tubing was made from drawn copper from the owners factory. This instrument was installed in All Saints Parish Church, Clayton-le-Woods, Lancashire in 1956.

All Saints Parish Church. Clayton-le-Woods, Lancashire

Great CC-C.61 notes		**Swell**		**Pedal** CCC-F.	
30 notes					
Open Diapason I	8'	Bourdon	16'	Open Diapason	16'
Open Diapason II	8'	Violin Diapason	8'	Bourdon	16'
Clarabella	8'	Viola d'Orchestra	8'	Octave	8'
Flute	4'	Rhor Flute	8'	Bass Flute	8'
Principal	4'	Principal	4'		
Twelfth	2 2/3'	Mixture	3rks		
Fifteenth	2'	Horn	8'		
Trumpet	8'	Oboe	8'		
		Tremulant			

Couplers
Swell to Great: Great to Pedal: Swell to Pedal: Swell Sub Octave:
Swell to Great Sub Octave: Swell Super Octave: Swell to Great Super Octave:
Great Sub Octave: Great Super Octave:

Accessories
3 Thumb pistons to Swell
3 Toe pistons to Swell
3 Thumb pistons to Great
3 Toe pistons to Great

Opening Recital. All Saints Parish Church. Clayton-le-Woods, Lancashire. June 13th 1956
Guest Organist. William Cliffe. LRAM. .A.R.C.O.,
Orchestral Leader. Albert H Bullock.
Dedication of Organ. – Hymn Praise My Soul The King Of Heaven.

Organ	*Toccata & Fugue in D minor*	J. S. Bach
Chorus	*Te Deum in B Flat*	Standford
Organ	*(a) Maytime A. Hollins. (b) Air & Variation*	M. Festing
Chorus	*The Heavens Are Telling (Creation)*	J. Haydn
Hymn	*Come Let Us Sing.*	
Organ	*Concerto No.5.* G.F. Handel *Andante - Allegro -Sicilliano - Allegro.*	
Hymn	*Bright The Vision.*	
Chorus	*Awake The Harp. (Creation)*	J. Haydn
Organ	*'The Swan' arr. by Guilmant*	Saint Saëns
Organ	*Toccata from Gothic Suite*	Boellman
Chorus	*Achieved Now Is The Glorious Work. (Creation)*	J. Haydn.
Hymn	*O Worship The King*	

There was now an increase in commissions and many of the older staff had settled back into civilian life after the war years, they, along with other members of the staff, have many amusing incidents to relate of their time with Messrs. Laycock & Bannister. Kenneth Seward had forty-years service with the firm, enlisted in the Royal Navy during 1942-45 and served on HMS 'Delphinium' a flower class corvette – Kenneth recalls an incident when he was on shore leave in Port Said. A call came for Able Seaman Seward to report back to repair the organ in the local church. Kenneth says – 'all I had was a screwdriver. I was told that, someone was waiting for me who would blow the organ. On arrival I found

Fig.52. The organ built for Mr. Henry Smith's residence 'Butterfield House' Bingley, Yorks. Removed to All Saints Church. Clayton-le-Woods, Messrs. Laycock & Bannister's First all electric console.

the problem was a weak spring on an old type of drawstop action which was causing a cipher (a note which is permanently sounding). The organblower turned out to be a dark skinned Arab in turban and flowing robes and adorned with two large daggers in his belt. I had no repair materials, so, resorting to organbuilders tricks; I approached the High Altar, broke off a piece of candle which nicely served to 'pack up' the offending spring. I also kept a watchful eye on the gentleman organblower with the two daggers'. Kenneth ends this story by saying 'I wonder if that candle is still packing up the weak spring'.

John Proctor, another long serving member and pipemaker, tells of visiting a Catholic Church where the organ was positioned high in the western gallery. The work required was a repair to the top of the swell box. John was working alone, but had procured an extension ladder in order to reach his destination. He then decided to obtain the services of the parish priest by asking if he would care to hold the ladder. The priest however, declined this invitation; as he felt unable to accept responsibility should the organbuilder have an accident by falling. He did promise however, that should this unfortunate occurrence arise, He would grant him 'absolution' on the way down.

Kenneth Seward, remembers tuning the organ at Bolton Abbey. He was working in a particularly confined position within the instrument, and shut down the blower as he eased himself between the building frame and casing, this awkward position caused his leg to become firmly trapped. Try as he might, he couldn't move. The apprentice who was helping at the keyboard became frightened and finally sent for the fire-brigade, who cut out a section of the framing. This incident was eventually picked up by the local radio 'talk show' and remained a long standing story at the Laycock & Bannister workshops for many years.

This smaller workshop purchased during the war years had been very active, with a large tuning area extending now into Scotland. Henry Bannister was now in semi-retirement and his son Frank was Managing Director. Commissions were forthcoming for new instruments and the rebuilding of others. It was time to move into larger premises and Mr. Frank Bannister obtained the Victorian Sunday School of St. John's, Main Street, Crosshills (now Keighley Road). This building had a handsome entrance porch leading into a large hall or erecting room laid out with workbenches around its sides. The adjoining rooms were re-used as stores and a voicing shop. On the first floor was the office, the galleries were provided with additional benches used for the making of wooden pipework, actions, rackboards etc. In the basement was the machine shop containing two circular saws, planing and morticing machines and some storage for timber.

Musical Opinion. March. 1967.[18]
"Messrs. Laycock & Bannister, Organbuilders of Crosshills, Yorkshire have recently removed into larger premises to facilitate the manufacturing, building and rebuilding of organs. The new premises also provide showroom space for demonstrating the new 'Coventry' series of electronic organs."

Fig. 53. Messrs. Laycock & Bannister's 'new' workshop Main Street, Crosshills, Yorks.

    The 'Coventry' series of electronic organs was pioneered by an electronics engineer named Pennal, for whom Messrs. Laycock & Bannister were agents for several years.

    In the time between the closure of the workshop in Aire Street and the removal into the 'new' premises, the company had a full order book which included the cleaning and renovation of the Grand Concert Organ in Huddersfield Town Hall. A large instrument built by Henry Willis consisting of 4 manuals and sixty-nine drawstops including couplers which was originally built for the Albert Hall, Newport, Monmouthshire in 1866.

    In 1880 it was offered for sale and purchased by Huddersfield Corporation. In 1891, Mr. Arthur Pearson. Mus.B. Oxon., FRCO, became Municipal Organist and arranged a series of winter concerts which were held in the Town Hall, at popular prices of 1d (one penny), 3d (threepence) and 6d (sixpence) respectively.

    Amongst the visiting artists was the eccentric concert organist David Clegg who held the position of organist at the Winter Gardens, Blackpool for many years. David Clegg used many 'gimmicks' to obtain his musical effects and some of this apparatus was brought along with him by an assistant. After one such concert given by Mr. Clegg. Arthur Pearson was approached by a man who said "Mr. Clegg played on a stop that you never play". "What sort of a stop was it"?

asked Mr. Pearson. "Well, it was like a fine bell" said the man. "Oh, Mr. Clegg took that stop home with him in his bag". replied Mr. Pearson. This in fact was what he had actually done.[19]

Other work from this 'new' workshop included

Haworth, Yorks, St. Michael's & All Angels PC	Rebuilding
Nelson, Lancs, St John's Parish Church	New organ
Leeds, Menston Methodist Church	New organ
Scotland, Dunoon, Holy Trinity Parish Church	New organ
Burnley, Lancs, St. Matthew's Parish Church	Rebuild
Scotland, Caithness, Wick. The Central Church	New organ
Ripon, Yorks, Holy Trinity Parish Church	New organ
Isle of Man, St. Olaves Parish Church	Rebuild
Hebden Bridge, Yorks. Old Town Church	Rebuild
Lancaster, Lancs, St. George's Parish Church	Rebuild
Arnside, Lancs, St. Mary's Parish Church	Rebuild
Haxby, Yorks Methodist Church	Rebuild
Skipton, Yorks. Ermysteads Grammar School	Rebuild
Scotland, Tayport, Queen Street Church.	Rebuild

The firm still continued to build within their own traditional style even when other companies were following the events of fashion, with the drastic re-casting of tonal choruses containing higher harmonics and the up-grading or modernising of the third manual (choir organ). The pattern usually adopted when a commission came into the workshop for re-building, particularly if it was one of their own instruments; was to restore to working and playing order without any drastic alterations. Fortunately there are now left for posterity a number of instruments by

Fig. 54. St John's Parish Church, Nelson. Lancashire. Built by Messrs, Laycock & Bannister, Crosshills Church now demolished and organ removed.

Photo. Laycock Bannister catalogue.

this firm in almost original condition.

Henry Bannister who had been in semi-retirement for several years but had continued to retain an interest in all that was going on at the workshop and in organ building in general died on May 23rd. 1967.[20]

Craven Herald & Pioneer, May, 23rd. 1967.
"Mr. Henry Bannister of 5 Breakmoor Avenue, Silsden died aged 77 years at 5 am on Tuesday morning. He was head of the Crosshills firm of Laycock and Bannister Organbuilders and is succeeded by his son Frank Bannister. Besides his son, Mr Bannister leaves a widow, who is President of the ladies' Section of Silsden Conservative Club. The funeral service was held at Skipton Crematorium."

The workshop still had a full order book and amongst the instruments in hand at this period included:
Bethesda Chapel, Elland, Yorks. New organ.
St. Michael and All Angels Parish Church, Whitley, Yorks. New organ.
Accrington Parish Church, Lancs. Rebuilding.
First Church of Christ Scientist, Halifax, Yorks. New organ.

The 'new' workshop in the town centre of Crosshills was run by a staff of eleven. The wage of an apprentice at that time

THE NEW CONSOLE

Fig 55. Bridlington Priory, Yorkshire. Installed 1968-9 by Messrs Laycock & Bannister Organbuilders, Crosshills, Yorkshire.

was £1-10s-0d per week. (£1.50p), an organbuilder received 17-5s-0d (£17.25p) per week (seven shillings and eight pence per hour) for a forty-five hour week, which included Saturday mornings. The workplace was active and not without certain amusing incidents. Benjamin Blackstone, a bench hand, working alone in St. Peter's Parish Church, Addingham, Yorks, was carrying out a small internal repair. As he shut off the wind in order to leave the organ the heavy top table of the reservoir dropped quickly, trapping his overalls and trousers. Tightly pinned to the side of the bellows his only means of escape was to struggle out of his clothes. His emergence from the organ case was accompanied by loud screams as the lady verger fled from the church. Benjamin hastily managed to switch on the blower in order to retrieve his trapped clothing.

Between 1968-69 the firm received what was arguably their largest undertaking; the commission to restore the famous Annessens instrument in Bridlington Priory, Yorkshire. The Priory was founded in 1113AD and at the Dissolution of the Monasteries was forfeited to the Crown. The Early English nave was spared as it formed the Parish Church, in order to leave somewhere for the people to worship.

Monsieur, Charles Annessens of Gramont, the finest organbuilder in Belgium in the second half of the 19th century; had erected several organs in Great Britain between 1880-90. The instrument he erected in Bridlington Priory consisted of three manuals and forty-one speaking stops; nine of which belonged to the pedal division. There was also a generous supply of orchestral tone colours by the inclusion of twelve reed stops. The total cost was £1,000.[21]

By the time of it's restoration by Laycock & Bannister this instrument had undergone some enlargement and the number of stops had increased to one-hundred including couplers. Most of the Annessens pipework was retained; but Messrs. Laycock & Bannister included several new ranks of pipes in their own style and also a new four manual detached drawstop console, which was placed on the north side of the choir.

From this period onwards the style of instruments from the Laycock & Bannister workshop began to change in order to meet a popular demand for more complete and brighter, if somewhat strident tonal choruses. There was now a demand for organs built on the extension system, which enabled the organbuilder to obtain two or more stops from a single rank of pipes. The firm built several instruments designed on this system and the demand for this type of organ lasted for some years. One of the first of these from the Crosshills workshop was installed in The Rodley Ecumenical Centre, Leeds in 1972; and from two ranks of pipework e.g. Diapason and Flute an instrument of sixteen stops could be produced. This method of construction brought a reduction in the amount of pipework, space and cost required but a loss in tonal quality.

Fate now took a hand in the history of the Firm with the deterioration in the health of it's Managing Director Mr. Frank Bannister who gave the members of his staff the first opportunity to purchase the company. This offer was not however taken up, but several outside parties did show considerable interest; and in 1973 Messrs. Nicholson & Co (Worcester) Ltd Organbuilders took control (Musical Opinion May 1974):[22]

Fig. 56. St Joseph's RC Church, Keighley, Yorkshire.

One of the first instruments under the new management was built for St. Joseph's Catholic Church, Keighley, Yorks: The church was completed in 1934 and is built in the Romanesque style on a magnificent scale.

The style of this new instrument is uncompromisingly neo-classical; with a Brustwerk division positioned below the Great or main organ, and based on a 2ft Principal rank. This department is enclosed behind folding doors which are hand operated. The tonal relationship between the two manual departments forms an agreeable musical balance. The Principal front pipes are made from polished copper. The limited Pedal organ of only two stops, both of which provides a musical foundation for either quiet registration or full chorus, where they may be augmented by coupling to the manuals. The action is mechanical throughout and the instrument is built within a free standing casework positioned just below the sanctuary area.

St. Joseph's Catholic Church. Keighley, Yorkshire

Messrs. Laycock & Bannister
Manual I. CC-C. 61 notes Manual II (Positive)

Principal	8' copper & tin	Gedact	8' wood
Rhorflute	8' metal	Koppelflote	4' plain metal
Octave	4' tin	Principal	2' tin
Sesquialtera	3-4rks tin	Quint	$1^{1}/_{3}$ tin
Mixture	2rks tin		

Pedal. CCC-g. 32 notes.

Couplers operated by Pedals
Positive to Great

| Bourdon | 16' walnut | Positive to Pedal |
| Fagott | 16' spotted metal | Great to Pedal |

Some seven months after the completion of the St. Joseph's instrument Messrs. Nicholson & Co (Worcester) were also taken over and the Laycock & Bannister branch went into the background although their name remained in use for certain tuning contracts.[23]

The Craven Herald & Pioneer. Friday, December 13th 1974 [24]
'Mr. Frank Bannister head of the Crosshills firm of organbuilders Laycock & Bannister, died aged sixty-six whilst visiting the home of friends. He had suffered from ill health for some years and had only recently left hospital. During his working life he was well known throughout the county of Yorkshire for the restoration of many church organs. He was a member of the Malsis Lodge of Freemasons, Crosshills and also a member of Crosshills Conservative Club and Keighley Golf Club."

The Crosshills workshop was finally closed but the fine building once a hive of organ building activity still stands on the main thoroughfare of the town (now in use as a supermarket). Messrs. Laycock & Bannister, one of the most prolific Yorkshire organbuilders of the 19th and 20th centuries was absorbed into the company of Nicholson Organbuilders of Worcester.

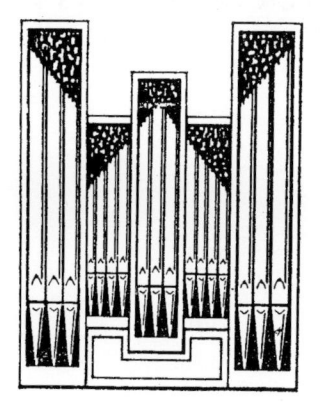

.... In the knowledge that co-operation brings considerable advantages to both organbuilders and clients, we are happy to announce that ....

LAYCOCK & BANNISTER
of Keighley, Yorks., England and Kirk Michael, Isle of Man
and
KENNETH JONES, LAYCOCK & BANNISTER
of Killalane, Glendalough, Bray, Co. Wicklow, Ireland

have formed an association for the building of high quality pipe organs in Britain, Ireland and overseas.

This association brings together

- DENNIS THURLOW whose tonal designs and voicing are very well known throughout these Islands and who has been in the forefront of the contemporary organ renaissance in England.

- KENNETH JONES whose particular field is in the design and finishing of classical organs, who has learned about durability and reliability the hard way through developing organbuilding in West Africa and who, complementary to organbuilding, is deeply involved in the musical life of Dublin as keyboard player and conductor.

- RAYMOND TODD who has vast experience in quality construction and first-class detailing, and to whom the quality and finish of what is *not* seen is as important as what *is* seen.

These complementary attributes enable the completion of instruments which are well made and above all musical. Our first choice in every situation is for tracker action, slider soundboards, a proper organ-case and balanced tonal design. We also rebuild and restore organs, where our creed is one of respect for the good work of the past. We believe that organ tone should be lively and interesting and with a musicality that will stand the test of time independently of fashion. We will not scale or voice to extremes, neither will we engage in the practice of "stock" scaling and voicing. Each instrument is scaled and voiced for its particular situation and energy requirements in relation to site cubic capacity. The association controls a considerable and experienced staff of craftsmen/organbuilders, many of whom are practising organists.

In the short time since our acquisition of the firm Laycock & Bannister and Kenneth Jones' return from West Africa our progress indicates that our policies, ideals and standards reflect the needs of discerning customers.

Chapter 3 Messrs. Laycock & Bannister
References

1. Census Records 1881. Leeds Central Library
2. Messrs. Laycock & Bannister Catalogue
3. Wm. Neville Blakey (Shop Books. Archive Collection.)
4. Ibid
5. Ibid
6. Scartop Sunday School & Chapel. Dennis Thompson
7. Wm. Neville Blakey (Shop Books. Archive Collection)
8. Ibid
9. Ibid
10. Ibid
11. Ibid
12. The Craven Herald & Pioneer. May 1919
13. Messrs. Laycock & Bannister Catalogue
14. The Craven Herald & Pioneer. December 13th. 1929
15. Wm. Neville Blakey (shop Books. Archive Collection)
16. The Craven Herald & Pioneer. December 1st. 1939
17. The Craven Herald & Pioneer. May 6th. 1960
18. Musical Opinion. March 1967
19. The Organ. Vol. IX. No.36 April 1930
20. The Craven Herald & Pioneer. May 23rd. 1967
21. Bridlington Priory (official Guide)
22. Musical Opinion. (Advertisement) 1974
23. Messrs. Nicholson & Co (Worcester) Organbuilders. (Letter to the author)
24. The Craven Herald & Pioneer. Friday December 13th. 1974

Photo W.Neville Blakey. Archive. Brierfield. Lancashire.

Fig.57. Frank Bannister and his wife Nora. Laycock & Bannister, Organ Builders, Crosshills, Keighley.

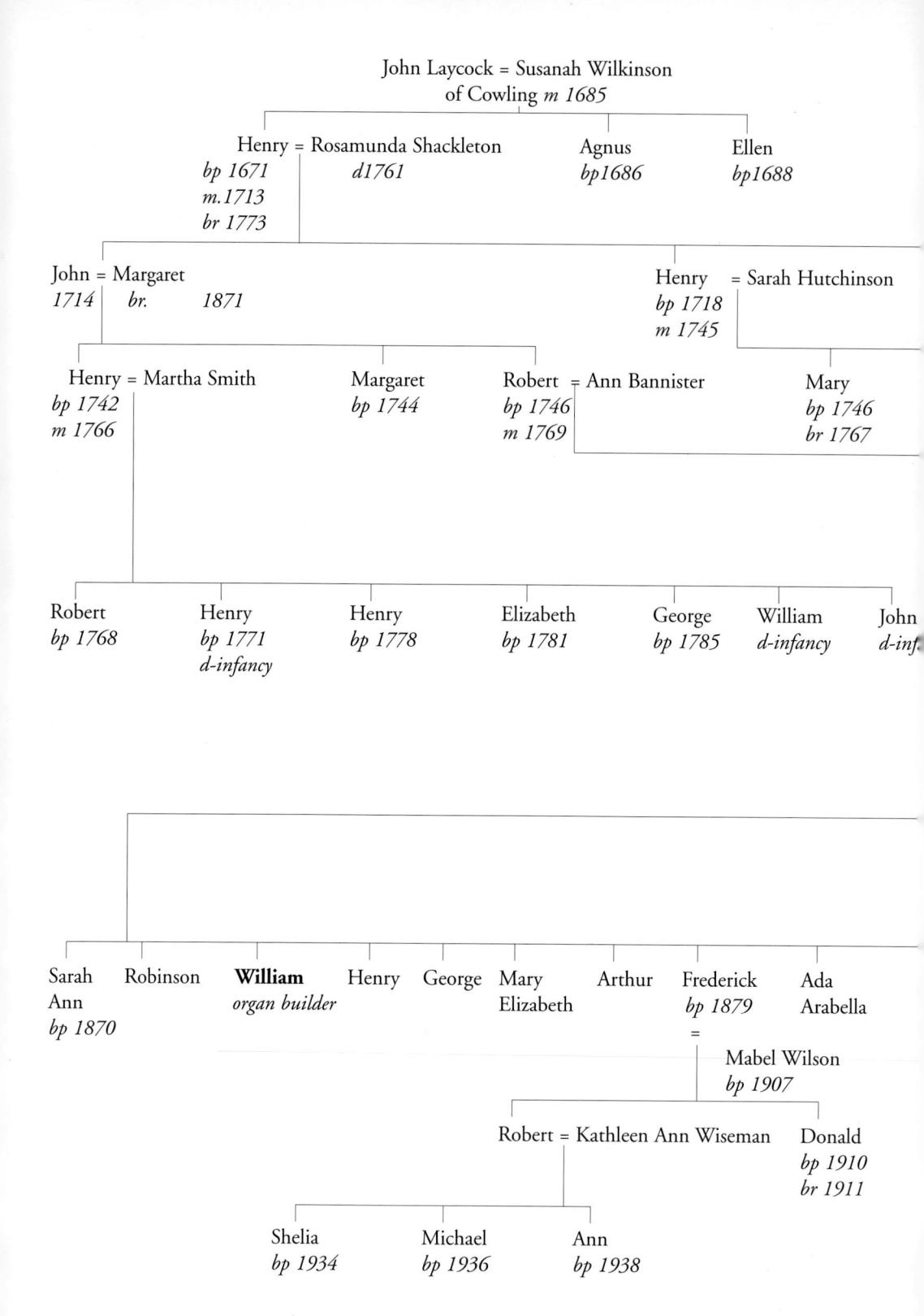

John Laycock = Susanah Wilkinson
of Cowling m 1685

Henry = Rosamunda Shackleton
bp 1671   d1761
m.1713
br 1773

Agnus
bp1686

Ellen
bp1688

John = Margaret
1714   br.   1871

Henry = Sarah Hutchinson
bp 1718
m 1745

Henry = Martha Smith
bp 1742
m 1766

Margaret
bp 1744

Robert = Ann Bannister
bp 1746
m 1769

Mary
bp 1746
br 1767

Robert
bp 1768

Henry
bp 1771
d-infancy

Henry
bp 1778

Elizabeth
bp 1781

George
bp 1785

William
d-infancy

John
d-inf.

Sarah
Ann
bp 1870

Robinson

William
organ builder

Henry

George

Mary
Elizabeth

Arthur

Frederick
bp 1879
=
Mabel Wilson
bp 1907

Ada
Arabella

Robert = Kathleen Ann Wiseman

Donald
bp 1910
br 1911

Shelia
bp 1934

Michael
bp 1936

Ann
bp 1938

94 John Laycock

Genealogy

bp = baptised
br = ???
d = died
m = married

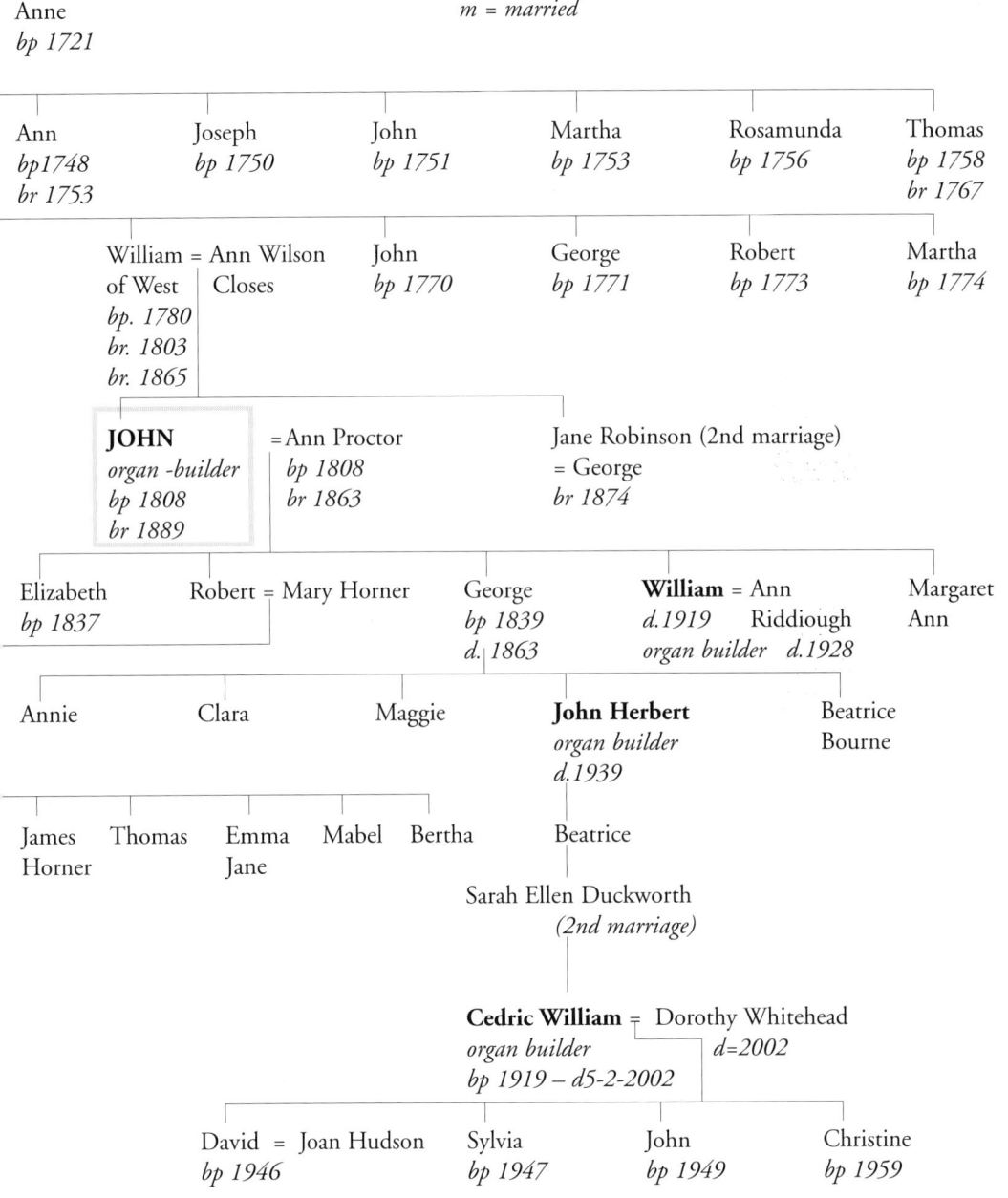

Anne
bp 1721

Ann	Joseph	John	Martha	Rosamunda	Thomas
bp 1748	bp 1750	bp 1751	bp 1753	bp 1756	bp 1758
br 1753					br 1767

William = Ann Wilson	John	George	Robert	Martha
of West Closes	bp 1770	bp 1771	bp 1773	bp 1774
bp. 1780				
br. 1803				
br. 1865				

JOHN = Ann Proctor   Jane Robinson (2nd marriage)
organ-builder   bp 1808   = George
bp 1808   br 1863   br 1874
br 1889

Elizabeth	Robert = Mary Horner	George	**William** = Ann	Margaret
bp 1837		bp 1839	d.1919 Riddiough	Ann
		d. 1863	*organ builder* d.1928	

Annie	Clara	Maggie	**John Herbert**	Beatrice
			organ builder	Bourne
			d.1939	

James	Thomas	Emma	Mabel	Bertha	Beatrice
Horner		Jane			

Sarah Ellen Duckworth
(2nd marriage)

Cedric William = Dorothy Whitehead
organ builder   d=2002
bp 1919 – d5-2-2002

David = Joan Hudson	Sylvia	John	Christine
bp 1946	bp 1947	bp 1949	bp 1959